INSIGHT AND VISION

Radoslav Andrea Tsanoff

INSIGHT AND VISION

Essays in Philosophy In honor of Radoslav Andrea Tsanoff

KONSTANTIN KOLENDA, Editor

VIRGIL C. ALDRICH

VAN METER AMES

CLIFFORD BARRETT

A. CORNELIUS BENJAMIN

GEORGE BOAS

JAMES STREET FULTON

A. CAMPBELL GARNETT

CHARLES HARTSHORNE

CHARLES W. HENDEL

CHARLES MORRIS

GLENN R. MORROW

PRINCIPIA PRESS OF TRINITY UNIVERSITY

SAN ANTONIO, TEXAS

The publisher gratefully acknowledges
the assistance of Sarah F. Eastman.

Printed in the United States of America
Library of Congress Catalog Card Number 66-16504

Foreword

In paying tribute to an outstanding member of our philosophical profession this collection of essays testifies also to the health and breadth of the contemporary scene in America. In these essays our authors continue to develop topics to which they have already made significant contributions. The high quality of their thought is again reflected on these pages. The reader will confront here philosophical reflection at its best: searching, committed, and vital. The title of this volume does not remain a mere aspiration.

The spirit in which our contributors participated in this joint effort to honor Professor Tsanoff is typified in the following response: "Naturally I am happy to accept your invitation. . . . During my entire professional life he has been one of the stars in my philosophical firmament, and it is reassuring to know that this star is still shining brightly. May it long continue to shine!" These sentiments are shared by many, many of us who, as Professor Tsanoff's students or colleagues, have learned to admire him as a man and as a philosopher.

The editor is grateful to all the contributors for their splendid cooperation on this project. He also wishes to make the following acknowledgments:

To Cambridge University Press for permitting Professor Benjamin to cite from C. P. Snow's *The Two Cultures: and A Second Look.*

To Humanities Press for permitting Professor Fulton to quote from Professor Tsanoff's *Worlds To Know.*

To Professor William G. MacLagan, Professor of Moral Philosophy at the University of Glasgow and Chairman of the Gifford Lectureship Committee, for allowing the publication of Professor Hendel's paper which partly overlaps material he had presented in his Gifford Lectures in 1962 and 1963, and which will appear in the printed version of the Lectures. While serving in the American Army University at Shrivenham, Oxford, in 1945, Professor Hendel discussed some ideas on the Philosophy of Politics with Professor Tsanoff and was encouraged by the latter to develop them full-scale. The paper on "Sovereignty and the Idea of Republic" represents a development of some of these early ideas and is illustrative of Professor Hendel's whole purpose in his Gifford Lectures.

We also wish to thank the *Rice University Studies,* and especially its editors, Professor Edward Norbeck and Professor Katherine Drew, for arranging for the publication of this volume; Mrs. Mimi Cohen for her painstaking and effective copy-editing; and Mrs. Gloria Weems for efficient secretarial help.

KONSTANTIN KOLENDA
Editor

Published Originally as Vol. 51, No. 4
Rice University Studies

INSIGHT AND VISION

Essays in Philosophy
In honor of Radoslav Andrea Tsanoff

RADOSLAV ANDREA TSANOFF

by James Street Fulton

Radoslav Andrea Tsanoff lectured to the first class in philosophy at the Rice Institute, then two years old, in 1914. A little more than fifty years later, in the spring of 1965, he was giving a brand-new course, on autobiography. In the meanwhile, Houston had grown from a brash, sprawling small city into a brash, sprawling megalopolitan center; Rice had passed from lusty infancy to confident maturity, changing its name along the way from Institute to University, in acknowledgement of the greatly increased demand for graduate and research programs; and the young Assistant Professor had become Emeritus Professor of Philosophy and Trustee Distinguished Professor of Humanities, a scholar of wide renown, almost a Texas institution.

The last phrase needs a word of explanation. His enthusiasm for everything momentous that men have achieved and can achieve artistically and intellectually and spiritually made him a cultural influence of singular force in the still provincial Southwest. Brilliant public lectures under Rice's auspices soon won him admirers far beyond the boundaries of the campus, just as his class lectures made friends and admirers of an ever-growing number of students. To this day he receives many more invitations than he can accept to speak before groups and meetings of all kinds. He has never condescended to an audience, but carefully writes out in advance what he is going to say, thereby expressing delicate ethical perception of the personal needs implied in an invitation to speak. His style, in speaking and in writing, reflects a mind at home in world literature and completely at ease in the highest intellectual company; but he talks to, never down to, his audience. Soon after coming to Rice, Tsanoff gave a series of public lectures which were published subsequently as an issue of the *Rice Institute Pamphlet* (in 1917) under the title, "The Problem of Life in the Russian Novel." Requests for copies were still being received more than forty years later. Equally outstanding, but in an entirely different context, was a talk given in the McCarthy era before a meeting called by the Rice Student Forum to consider the problem of intellectual freedom in view of certain current ideas and activities of a repressive character. While other speakers dealt with current controversies, Tsanoff rose at once above the momentary to the abiding principles of the American faith. His statement of what our country stands for and strives to make actual was so affirmative, so direct, so simple, so artlessly eloquent that those who heard him were lifted out of their seats in spontaneous ovation. What he did at that moment revealed the philosopher: he stood with the others and joined in the ovation. It was clear to him that not he but the idea of America had inspired the outburst of enthusiasm. With humility he saw himself as the servant of this idea, the instrument through which it could speak; so he disclaimed personal credit for his utterance.

The communication of ideas outside the academic community is a natural extension of the life of a scholar. Tsanoff exerted a powerful, constructive influence on the larger community in other ways as well, as is instanced by his service for twenty-eight years on the Board of Directors of the Houston Symphony Society. Especially during early years, when it was engaged in a relentless struggle for existence, he grappled energetically with the emergencies, even helping to canvass possible contributors by phone. For eight years he was also a Trustee of the Houston Museum of Fine Arts.

While in these and other ways the duties of a citizen and neighbor were being ungrudgingly discharged, his real work was being done in the scholar's study. A bare glance at the bibliography listed elsewhere in this volume will give an idea of the fruitfulness of the countless hours spent there. Titles alone cannot be expected to reveal the erudition, the discriminating judgment, the mastery of balance and rhythm, which make one page after another noteworthy in many essays and books. By virtue of these accomplishments and the force of his personality, Tsanoff for decades personified philosophy to Rice and Rice to the philosophical world. I shall venture a little later to give a broad indication of the philosophy that inspires his writing and informs his life.

For the present I wish to emphasize that absorption in his own creative work never prevented or delayed his discharge of other duties to the institution which he served. He always carried a full teaching load, usually with large classes, and never in his whole career had the assistance of a reader. He served efficiently on committees, including the time-consuming Committee on Examinations and Standing, of which he was a member for sixteen years. And, most significantly, he for forty-two years built the philosophy holdings in the library, from two volumes in 1914 to the excellent collection that with little more than routine additions will support the research activities of a growing department throughout the future. During those years, he was also administratively responsible for Philosophy, for Education, for Psychology. Those who know the distractions of such complex duties wonder how he did so much.

Perhaps, it was because he never was supplied a secretary.

One morning, a few years after his retirement, Tsanoff came briskly into the corridor that Philosophy and English then shared in Anderson Hall. It could not have been later than eight-thirty. As usual he had risen early and gotten in a couple of hours of work, and now had driven eleven miles through heavy traffic, eager for the day he had planned at his desk in the library. He was even more cheerful than usual, a little excited, almost gay, when he fell upon a colleague in the English Department who specialized in nineteenth century romanticism. "Will," he said, "I don't know how it came about; but as I was driving in this morning, two whole cantos of *Childe Harold* went through my mind." That he could recite yards of Byron seemed perfectly natural to him (why, he had learned it as a schoolboy in Bulgaria); that he did so on that occasion surprised him, and he was unaffectedly delighted with the experience.

A prodigious memory may become a curse by inexorably storing trivia or by interfering with thought. Tsanoff never exposed his mind to the cheap or meretricious. He disciplined his great gift by exercising it on the highest products of human genius and by subordinating it to a controlling philosophical purpose. The vastness of his learning is focused and refracted by an active mind onto the pages of his works and built into the texture of his daily life. Affirmatively, it places at his almost instant disposal great insights of genius in at least eight languages —from simple folk wisdom to sublime religious utterances. Negatively, it forms an absolute bulwark against one-eyed wisdom, rigid factionalism, sectarian simplification. Tsanoff is too constantly aware of alternatives to be fanatic. His mind always sees a balance among claims that he knows have been passionately advanced and masterfully defended against each other, for balance is the dynamic equivalent of the ultimate stability: integrity of purpose and style, which the mind pursues as its demanding goal and satisfying destiny. This live integrity matures not eclectically by gathering this and that snippet of presumed wisdom, but teleologically by arduously respecting the superiority of the inherently superior.

One of his most recently published books, *Worlds to Know,* well illustrates the spirit of his philosophy and his life. I can do no better than quote at some length from its concluding pages, where the author is himself summarizing his guiding conviction, indeed his life's work so far:

> Our modern specialized and often onesided thinking has found expression in the over-departmentalized organization of our universities. We need greater integration in our programs of higher education. Any real basic problem is bound to lead our research beyond our departmental bailiwick. In my own experience, at least, I have found that this is especially true in philosophy. In

studying the belief in immortality, the problem of evil, the ways of genius, I was again and again led from "straight philosophy" into religion, into history and literature, psychology and other sciences. Real problems pay no attention to departmental fences; they go their ways, and in following their various courses one may learn the importance of integrative thinking.

Our philosophy should not be the philosophy of a school. It must not be dictated by conformity to any preconceived formula, but must itself be the integration of various evidence and inference that leads to the confirmation or to the revision of traditional and provisional formulae. For this is always the advantage of sound philosophical interpretation, that in its critical integrating outlook many special ideas reveal significant aspects or inferences which they do not manifest when regarded solely in their special provinces. Ideas become more cultivated; their meaning expands and mellows when they enter into the stimulating society of more thorough and balanced reflection.[1]

But what ideas, specifically, had "become more cultivated" in his experience? Again, he has said it himself:

The view of the World as Drama is the most characteristic outlook on the Reality of Values. Here man's intelligence—reason and feeling and spiritual vision—contemplates its own creative activity up to the verge and summit of genius. Corresponding to the factual interplay of causes and urges and reasons and purposes across the vast span of cosmic perspectives which we have been endeavoring to understand, the dramatic outlook reveals the strains in the life of spiritual aspiration, the counterplay of ideals in the pursuit of perfection and in the struggle with evil.

The perspective of the world as process at this distinctively spiritual level manifests a dynamic of values. The world as drama is a gradation of higher and lower satisfactions and purposes and ideals. Value is never simply there, to be described or explained. It enters the stage of possible realization as a challenge and an aspiration, or as a menace or an insidious lure. The entire realm of values is one of striving or relapse, achievement or frustration, perfection or degradation. For here on the highest reaches of reality, man is ever resisting the drags of his lower nature or yielding to them. In social activities progress appears dubious when so often man's reason itself is bedeviled to serve lower impulses, to make him "beastlier than any beast," in the words of Goethe's Mephistopheles. Artistic creation is so often checked or misdirected by confusion or vulgarity. The moral life is itself a dramatic contest of values and purposes, arduous in the struggle between aspiration and appetite, baffling in the tragic choice between counter-evils. These are gray and grim aspects of the spiritual life, and religion has expressed them in its emphasis on man's sinfulness and his utter need of redemption. The religious gospel of salvation is a gospel of hope, hope to contrite man. The parable of the Prodigal Son evidences this dual conviction. The prodigal son is the son of his Father—but a prodigal son.

Have we presented the dramatic perspective of the world of values in a dour pessimistic regard? It has also its vistas of more positive and sublime achievement. In our other views of the world—as cosmic mechanism, or evolution or history—we have been considering the varieties and the complexity and the limits of available knowledge. Now we contemplate man's paths towards wisdom, so frequently uncertain, unmarked and untrodden, so limitless in their forward reach, onward and upward. Here man's creative spirit surpasses itself, so often by not being subservient to cautious reason, but not by an initial dismissal of reason. How wisely St. Thomas Aquinas counselled his theological doctors: Go with reason as far as it takes you, in its right direction; faith will then take you the rest of the way. In many fields of spiritual activity this same basic wisdom has been expressed. So Pasteur affirmed that the great creative ideas come to minds that have been prepared for them by thorough inquiry. And Poincaré: After having tried really hard, stop trying, and it will achieve itself. From scaling the ideal heights, will some of my readers turn to plain mountain climbing? On the slippery trails inexperienced foolhardiness may prove fatal. But repeatedly the seasoned climber comes to a step of precarious outcome, where only a resolute leap can sway the possible odds between success and disaster. The lower ramparts of achievement may be reduced by plodding reflection, but eventually genius must storm the citadels of perfection. The fuller truth, however, requires that we write this last sentence also in the reverse order, so as to include the recognition of the superlative capacity for hard work.[2]

The bare facts of Tsanoff's academic biography are hardly a respectable shadow of the vital substance, but may be included for the sake of the record. He was born in Sofia, Bulgaria, January 3, 1887. His father was an author, educator, and newspaper editor, and young Radoslav grew up in the security of a strong family, which shared and prized the high literary and intellectual heritage of all Europe. When at fifteen he looked for further education beyond the borders of his Balkan homeland, he did not turn, as one might expect, to the powerful nations of Europe or to England, but to the United States. In this he was following his father, who had studied at Cornell University as a young man. The fifteen-year old prepared for America by spending a year at Robert College, the American school in Constantinople. In 1903 he entered Oberlin College in Oberlin, Ohio, completed his undergraduate course with distinction in three years, and proceeded to Cornell University for his doctor's degree, which he received in 1910.

With the exception of the first two years, spent at Clark University, in Worcester, Massachusetts, a strange interlude at Shrivenham American University in Berkshire, England, in 1945, several visiting professorships, and, after retirement, two years as M. D. Anderson Professor of Philosophy at the University of Houston, Tsanoff's entire professional career is identified with Rice, where since 1961 he has held an appointment as Trustee Distinguished Professor of Humanities.

His marriage in 1912 to a Cornell co-ed, Corrinne Stephenson, was enduringly a spectacular success, yielding two talented daughters, four handsome grandsons, and, at last count, two great-grandchildren. Mrs. Tsanoff, in addition to the myriad activities of wife, mother and grandmother, hostess, and leader in community service, has typed all her husband's manuscripts and staunchly assisted him in the dreadful chore of seeing book after book through the press.

Let that suffice.

I hope I shall be forgiven a final, very personal indulgence. I cannot close this piece without acknowledging my gratitude to Radoslav Tsanoff for his friendship, his selfless support, his unfailing encouragement, his remarkable example. In twenty years of constant close association I have known him indignant but never ill-tempered, hurried but never impatient with persons in need of him, always courteous but never *merely* courteous, always generous, never mean. After running the Department for more than forty years, he has shown almost superhuman restraint in not offering his successor a single piece of unsought advice; but he has always been ready instantly to drop whatever of his own he was doing if I sought his help and counsel. Radoslav Tsanoff, the man, has taught me more than he will ever put in books.

Not only on the lives of his friends but on the character of Rice University he has left his indelible signature. He has solved, in practice if not theory, the problem of a significant "objective immortality."

NOTES

1. Radoslav A. Tsanoff, *Worlds to Know: A Philosophy of Cosmic Perspectives.* (New York, 1962), pp. 215-216. (English edition entitled *Science and Human Perspectives* [London, Routledge & Kegan Paul].)
2. *Op. cit.*, pp. 213-215.

SELF-CONSCIOUSNESS

by Virgil C. Aldrich

The instructions, "Don't be so self-conscious," "You should be more conscious of yourself," and the like, are interpreted in a variety of ways, depending on the context. On the one hand, there are what may be called the popular or practical interpretations, and on the other, the more sophisticated or theoretically complicated ones. Let me glance first at some examples of the practical sort in a by-passing manner, since I am interested primarily in the other kind.

You are at a cocktail party for some dignitary and discover that a quantity of hors d'oeuvre dip has been on your beard for some time. You become painfully self-conscious, with the form of self-consciousness called embarrassment. Or you are a wallflower at the party, not because you are homely in appearance, but because you are shy. Shyness is a built-in, self-negating sort of self-consciousness that tends to keep the shy person out of circulation in social situations, perhaps because of an unfavorable estimate of himself. Or you may suffer from narcissism, being in love with yourself, in a sort of introverted and romantic preoccupation with the image of your self, and this too would tend to keep you out of the social whirl at the party. Or, opposite to all these cases, you might be an exhibitionist, self-conscious in a way that puts your self on exhibit at every turn, compulsively. This also might get you ostracized, in the end.

Such examples could easily be multiplied beyond necessity, and I do not want to do that. The point is that in all such cases I could properly tell you not to be so self-conscious, and you and everybody else concerned would quite readily get the sense of the instruction, in those situations and the like. However, I can't refrain from mentioning one more example. Suppose you are an exhibitionist in the above sense and are playing a part in a play on stage. Your job as an actor is to engage in a pattern of actions—including speaking, which is the most essential and expressive human action of all—that best exhibits the person of the character you are playing, not your own person or self. This requires a studied awareness of the pattern of actions which is the medium of the dramatic art. Now if you here make the mistake of being aware of yourself instead, or of putting yourself on exhibit as well, thereby drawing attention away from the character you are playing, the admonishment, "Don't be so self-conscious," would again apply. Similar remarks hold for the writer whose style is, as we say, "self-conscious," out of too much concern on the part of the author to make a show of his own virtuosity at literary composition, at the expense of what he is supposed to be portraying in the linguistic medium of his art.

As for the positive instruction, "You should be more conscious of yourself," it too has practical interpretations and applications like the negative one I've been illustrating. One might direct it at a man with bad table manners—"Be more conscious of yourself, watch yourself!" —or to one who tends impulsively to give away things that the recipients do not need as much as the giver does. But, since it is this positive sort of instruction that readily lends itself to the more *theoretically* involved or sophisticated interpretation I mentioned above and which is the chief concern of this essay, I turn from the popular to the philosophical usages. Of course, the negative instruction, "Don't be so self-conscious," can be taken this way also. The philosophical mystic, for example, has quite some use for this, but what he makes of it, as we shall see, is very different from what has been made of it in the above cases. Be all this as it may, let us attend in what follows to the positive instruction, "You should be more conscious of yourself," as an occasion to examine what I have called the theoretically involved interpretations, treating these as if they express the kind of philosophical self-consciousness that prevailed at the time. So I proceed with the attempt to give you a bird's-eye view of the history of some of these philosophies of self-consciousness. These, unlike the practical or popular uses of the injunctions to be or not to be self-conscious, involve some analysis of self-consciousness, and of course this will involve a theory of the self and its self-consciousness. I want the brief story I am going to tell you of this to impress you with the evolutionary continuity or development of this concept, through the various theories in chronological order.

First, of course, Socrates, because as formulated by Plato, he *is* first. In Socrates' heyday, the Sophists were propagating a popular and easy sort of subjectivism and scepticism, the sort that the sophomore annoys his parents with after a year of college. Not that the *arguments* of the great Sophists for such a view were nearly as immature as the sophomore's. They were so penetrating that they taxed Socrates' powers of refutation to the limit. Protagoras, for example, argued the proposition that man is the measure of all things. *Each* man is the measure of reality and truth. To become conscious of one's self was, for Protagoras, to become conscious of the fact that it was a subjective or small container of everything knowable by him. It was this idea of the self and self-consciousness that Socrates had to attack. As Plato's hero, he finally emerged with the notion, systematically argued, that what is subjective or private to the self is not at all essential to it. What is essential to it and its salvation is the consciousness of certain eternal objects to which *any* rational mind has access, in the sort of intellectual contemplation that the Platonic Socrates identified with knowledge. This tended to empty the self of its subjective contents in favor of consciousness of an objective reality that transcends private experience. Thus, realizing oneself was conceived as the intellectual love of timeless and selfless objects, and this absorption into eternal entities, by abstract contemplation, makes the self immortal. So the Socratic injunction, "Know thyself," turns out, paradoxically, to require the particular self to lose itself in a reality that lies beyond the self. True self-consciousness, philosophically arrived at, thus involves the paradox of self-realization through the absorption of the self into something selfless, something in which the identity of the particular self, as *subject* of the experience, is lost. The self as subject and subjective is a mere appearance, not ultimately real.

The note sounded here is not unlike that of the later Christian teaching concerning the self and its salvation. There too is the paradox of the self dying unto itself, though this time more by faith and love than by knowledge or the exercise of reason. (Plato too had said that philosophy is learning how to die.) But the Christian orthodox teaching places more emphasis on selfhood as ultimate; I don't want to stress this at this point of the story. Rather, it is the echo that Platonism got in subsequent mysticism, beginning with Plotinus, that I next draw your attention to. In so far as Christian doctrine is mystical, it will be implicitly included in this notice. So I turn to mysticism.

According to the mystic, a sustained and educated effort at self-consciousness will not only make the particular self vanish into nothingness in the end, but, in the white radiance of that experience, it will become clear that the self was really nothing all along, even in the beginning. Its apparent being will dissolve away into its real nonbeing. This is the mystical experience. Since this pilgrim's progress of the soul is pictured as a passage from appearance to reality, the nonbeing into which it finally sinks, losing its identity like a drop of water in the ocean, is judged to be a blessed event—the new birth of the self through its annihilation. Here again is the paradox of consummating the self by annihilating it. The Oriental mystic has compared this to pouring milk into milk. Paraphrasing a passage in the *Brahma Sutra,* the particular self is an *apparent* modification of an ultimate *x*. The illusion of this particular modification called the self is produced, according to the passage, by the self's unfortunate linguistic activities. It uses language, names, and the concepts that go along with these. It is this that makes it look as if there really are many particular things including the self, deployed in time and space. The truth is that these linguistic concoctions are mere appearances carved out of an absolute, undifferentiated unity that is nameless and ineffable, realized only in mystical experience and about which the wise man, the true seer, will keep mum. The current verbal practices of Zen Buddhism, with its *koans,* are aimed at driving home this point—breaking through the logical web of language.

So the instruction, "You should be more conscious of yourself," turns out, in this context of theoretical interpretation, to be issued in the hope that the self you only seem to be, as an illusory, verbal construct, will finally be rejected as full of sound and fury, signifying nothing. Or, if you are a self-seeking sort of person, the mystic might as well say to you, "Don't be so self-conscious," and his meaning will be clear in the context of his mysticism.

Now make with me a big jump out of this cosmic, anti-rational mood into the scientific ethos that emerged in the West in the sixteenth century and jelled in the seventeenth. We find there that particular selves, as subjects of subjective experience, get recognized with a bang, not a whimper; but for rather embarrassing reasons. In fact, all bona fide experience begins to look subjective or "inner" in this new Light of Nature that, for the first great scientists of this period, revealed the external or outer world only as mechanically and mathematically structured. Moreover, it made this outer realm of matter look more real than the inner subjective realm of mind. It was in this age that the great dualism between mind within, and matter without, emerged with a vengeance. It became systematic in Descartes' *Meditations,* whose hero was his older contemporary Galileo, and fifty years later in John Locke who spoke reverently of "the incomparable Mr. Newton."

Under the impact of the new scientific world-picture, there seemed to be no place for mind-with-its-animation in the real external world in space and time. Space, said Descartes, is the essence of matter, and mind has no spatial properties at all. It is nowhere at all. Thus it has no affinity, no kinship, with the real external world of nature, in space. Thus it is not really possible for the self as mind to take the plunge of mystical experience out of itself into the vast ocean around it of the Not-Self. Thus each self is stuck with itself, confined to its own subjective contents. Strictly speaking, it has no direct experience of anything but these subjective contents or psychological states. Even its clearest and most distinct ideas that are put to work in its most responsible mental operations called scientific research are subjective. We must *assume* that these, when mathematically formulated, correspond to the skeletal realities of the external world, but, as Descartes argued, we do not *know* that there is any such correspondence without a supernatural guarantee. And it was precisely the concept of the supernatural that was getting its props knocked out from under it by the new scientific world-picture. Descartes had to resort to nonscientific arguments for God's existence in a desperate effort to keep the supernatural on its props despite the swelling tide of scientific naturalism. He did this because God alone could save natural knowledge from the swelling tide of scepticism.

Since only abstract, mathematical thinking had some chance of achieving true correspondence with reality external to mind, the doctrine of the sheer subjectivity of all sense-perceptual, imaginative and spiritual experience emerged with a new force. These are just so much smog compared with the scientific metrics of clear and distinct concepts. Thus, curiously, the new science tended to agree with the old mysticism on one count. The self is chock full of illusory and misleading appearances that simply must be seen through if there is to be anything like an approximation to knowledge and truth. (Bacon's idols of the mind.) But, according to the new science, the emotional escape in mystical experience from these deceptive appearances that mystics of India call *maya* is not really possible. The mystical experience is a lapse, a fall, from intellectual grace; not a salvation. Having it only augments the illusion. Or even just trying to have it.

So, in this brave new world, the injunction, "Know thyself," or, "You should be more conscious of your self," is a warning not to be taken in by its "subjective contents" that have no chance of objective correspondence with the demented external world of mechanical happenings under geometrical and causal laws. But even the mathematical ideas by which you have a better chance of achieving such correspondence are subjective contents of the self. So it is still by a selective kind of introspection that you *may* come to know something outside the self, i.e., by attending to its most clear and distinct subjective contents. To put the matter tersely, one may say that, according to this way of thinking and theorizing about the self, self-consciousness is inescapable. You can't help being self-conscious. You never really have direct access to, or get directly at, anything but the subjective contents of your self or mind, whether in perception or conception. Your own impressions and ideas are all you ever encounter anywhere in the field of your experience and thought. You are caught in the inner privacy of yourself, and not even a Houdini can get out of *this* trap.

By the middle of the eighteenth century, the Scottish sceptic David Hume had driven home the negative implications of this new dualism. The embryo of scepticism curled in its womb was brought to light and maturity by his treatment. We do not experience things, but only our impressions of things. And all our ideas, comprising such knowledge as we have, derive from just these impressions, not from things. Even mental things like ourselves or minds are not directly experienced. Only certain impressions of them are, impressions that *suggest* they must belong to something called self or mind. (Nobody ever simply sees or hears or feels his own mind per se, or any other.) Just as other impressions *seem* to be connected with material things outside the mind. So, strictly speaking, instead of *knowledge* of things either material or mental, there are only pseudo-ideas of these. The genuine ideas, deriving from impressions only, reveal only the kinds and orders of impressions. Not of things, either material or mental. The rest is just sheer guesswork under psychological laws of association of ideas, not knowledge. The term "guesswork" here is due to Bertrand Russell, who also was a sceptic in one of the stages of his development. In short, both subjectivism and objectivism are hamstrung as meaningless, by Hume's analysis, if subjectivism involves a claim to knowledge of the self that *has* the impressions.

After Hume had done his work, or if I may play with his pet term, made his "impression" on the mind of the eighteenth century, it was clear that if there is anything like a game of knowledge-of-things to be played and won, some philosopher with a new angle, or a hitherto unplayed card up his sleeve, would have to sit down to the conceptual poker table. Someone who had absorbed the scientific ethos through the pores and, while understanding and respecting it, had premonitions of another ethos to come. Someone who would find intolerable what the sceptic had done to the age-old maxim, "Be conscious of your self" ("Know thyself"). If Hume was right, it was impossible to obey it. The best one could do to preserve one's sanity, after trying hard to obey it, was to follow Hume's own example, You stop trying, and turn for relief to play a game of backgammon—which, like poker, is also a game of chance. As is the game of knowledge.

Another thing was also clear at this stage. The self or the mind had by this time a big premium on it, though it had been used as a waste-basket to contain human values and purposes that had no place in the executive order of the external world. The evolution of thought from Descartes to Berkeley, who was just before Hume, had involved a retreat into the inner realm of mind from the outer realm of material things. Thus had things been subjectified into contents of the mind, in so far as any experience or knowledge of them is at all possible. Now, if by "the mind" here you mean *your* mind, then you are a solipsist, and such a view simply won't do. The solipsist argues that only he and his self-contained world really exist. Of such a view even the sceptic Hume had said that, though it admits of no refutation, yet it produces no conviction. But I think we have an informal sort of refutation in the whimsical story about the French solipsist who complained, in a letter to Bertrand Russell, that nobody *else* would accept his excellent arguments showing that only *he,* the Frenchman, exists. Even the solipsist needs the company of other selves, when he argues. If he has any argument at all. So solipsism is self-refuting. The notion of arguing with oneself will not help here, since one cannot argue with himself until he has learned to argue, and this one does at first with another self.

Nevertheless, the self had by this time become the focal point on which the being of anything knowable and experienceable seemed to depend. How then to reinstate things as genuine and public objects of experience and knowledge "out there," without abandoning the notion of their containment by, and dependence on, a self or mind? That is, by replacing the false subjectivism with a true one? A formula for this had to be found as the only way out of the cramp of the new emphasis on the privacy of the experience of each-little-self-unto-itself.

Kant and the German romanticists after him found the formula and worked it with a vengeance, beginning in the latter part of the eighteenth century and on up to the middle of the nineteenth. I shall be atrociously short about this development, with some pangs of conscience. The formula is: enlarge the self into the Absolute Self or Mind, and let your self and mine be finite parts of it, with Absolute Mind as their real essence. Then there will again be an objective—this time spiritual—environment for our selves containing public realities independent of my self and yours, and to be experienced and known by us when our experiencing and thinking is responsible. The disciplines that make these responsible and adequate to the task of coping with this spiritual reality are the humanities, not the sciences. Not even the science of pure mathematics. The blessing, indeed salvation, of true insight into the nature of things comes most effectively through the arts, especially literature, with poetry as the essence, more essential even than religion, though this too is more revealing than science. But, you will say, these humanistic disciplines are subjective expressions of imagination and feeling. Of course they are, and that precisely is why they serve the purpose of understanding and knowledge of the real world better than the intellectual abstractions of scientific investigation. You must remember that we live, move, and have our being in the Absolute Self, an all-inclusive Subject or Mind. That is why the subjective disciplines are on top, in the hierarchy of the disciplines. One properly goes up, ascends, to them, and down to the derivative and deteriorated view of things in the sciences. The sciences are at the bottom, concerned as they are with abstractions that make the spiritual realities around us look like inanimate and mechanical objects. To shake off such illusions, one turns advisedly, say, to

Tintern Abbey for Wordsworth's reminder that we are in The Presence. Or to Hegel's philosophy of the World Spirit.

In philosophy, this sort of anti-scientific world-view waned after—even before—Schopenhauer's death in 1860. It had a sort of revival through the turn of the century in British, American, and Italian Neo-idealism, and then again ceased to have much influence. It is in this quiescent state at present, though you can still feel its pulse if you put your finger in the right places—on those few individuals who are functioning as a saving remnant in honor of one of the great traditions in philosophy.

But what about the interpretation of our imperatives of self-consciousness in the context of such a theory? There they tended to feature the all-pervasive Absolute Ego, one way or another. The main point was that our finite, fluctuating selves, our little selves, tend to coalesce with this larger Self, even to *be* it, when they think and act as responsibly as they can. In fact, such conduct *is* the activity of the same Larger Self within us all. So it becomes important for us to be or realize this great potential, in the consciousness that this is what we ultimately are, our real being. Thus the instruction, "Don't be so self-conscious," would read, "Don't be so aware of (so stuck with) the little self that you really are not." And, "Be more conscious of your self, know thyself," would go, "Become aware of the Larger Self you most truly are." Since all this draws attention to real *being*—or has "ontological import"—such imperatives were boiled down into the single "Be yourself!" "*Sei was du bist!*" Your real self. What you really are. Self-consciousness of this expanding and more and more inclusive sort, that progressively reveals the Absolute Self as its essence, was the theme with variations in the romantic movement. Philosophically speaking, it culminated in Hegel in the first half of the last century. Its literary expression took on many forms, including that of the "existential mood" in which the great Russian novelists also participated. In this form, darkened with the tragic consciousness of what it is to be a man, the romantic spirit is still quite alive and to be reckoned with, even in communist Russia. Remember Pasternak, ostracized by The Party for his heresy of the anti-scientific world-view expressed in his poetry. (His novel *Dr. Zhivago* was also a poem, plainly against the machinations—and I mean also the "machine-ations" of The Party—of dialectical materialism.)

Now, in quick retrospect, you can see that the story has been of a tendency at first, in the early Greek period and subsequent mysticism, to lose the self in what is wholly Not-Self; and then, in the modern scientific and subsequent romantic period, the tendency either to get stuck sceptically with the little self or to escape from this by finding the self in the world of the true, Larger Self. (The term "larger self" is, by the way, due to Harvard's Josiah Royce, in his heyday at the turn of our century.) In short, the picture we get, in retrospect, is of two mighty opposites: non-subjectivism against subjectivism. (I say "non-subjectivism" instead of "objectivism" because, e.g., mysticism is non-subjectivistic but not objectivistic. Indeed, it denies the reality of any objects, including Plato's eternal Forms.)

An impartial yet deeply concerned view of this impasse, activated by the question, "Which view is the right one?" has, mainly in the last thirty-five years, generated a new kind of philosophical self-consciousness, a language-consciousness. Indeed, the predicament required it, as the next new angle or card to be played if the game was not to be abandoned at the dead end it had reached. At this time, philosophical self-consciousness began to emerge as language-consciousness. The feeling grew among the philosophers that they had unconsciously had their say out of selves and worlds structured by the linguistic forms they were using and being used by. "Linguistic" here does not mean what it means to linguists or to lexicographers. It has a deeper meaning that does greater justice to the power of language to order the realm in which a man, as a man, is active, stylizing everything he does even when he is not *actually* using the language. This notion of language as a constitutive form, a form of life, modifying things even in the field of perception, not just conception, now has currency among language philosophers in quite different camps. (Even Heidegger in existentialism and Merleau-Ponty in phenomenology.) Notice the curious agreement here with the ancient mystic's view of language. The mystic had also asserted the power of language to create and order the world of diverse things that every man is aware of. But for the mystic this was not reality. Reality was the undifferentiated continuum or unbroken unity back of the multiple appearances. So he rejected language. Not so the new philosophers of language. For them, discarding language is throwing the baby out with the bath, since, as Waismann said, reality is realized in the forms of language-in-action, as character is in a face or in a pattern of human actions, of which language-using is the greatest and most refined. Man is best defined as a language-using animal—*animal symbolicum*—since his language is the soul of him. It is this that distinguishes him from the other animals. Moreover, it is this that distinguishes between kinds of men, both culturally speaking and according as they are primarily scientists or artists or religious people or simply men of action. The language of science is the soul of the scientist, the language of poetry of the poet, and so on. Thus there is a need for a nonspecial or neutral account of all these in their various relationships, bringing to light the logical grammar of each, formal and informal, and it is the philosopher's job to adopt this new spirit of high neutrality and use language in a nonspecial way in the account. It is not an easy job because such neutrality must be highly disciplined or cultivated if it is to bear fruit.

My story—my plot, if you like—has had a beginning and a middle. You can feel that it has been ending through the last page or two. I shall say "period" to it by finally mentioning a few names with the related key ideas, all in this new linguistic ethos.

It was Cassirer who, in his philosophy of symbolic forms, got beyond the traditional dialectical idealism by giving it a twist that has been called Neo-Kantian. Kant's idealism had been more critical and cautious than Hegel's, so has had more influence on the developments I am now speaking of, in the end. Cassirer made much of the language of myth, of art, of science, of religion, treating these as symbolic forms that structure autonomous worlds under different criteria of intelligibility. Thus did he multiply the constitutive forms of life and its "objects" beyond the few that Kant recognized or ever dreamt of in his philosophy. Concurrently, the logical positivist Carnap—who, by the way, like Cassirer, began as a continental European—drew a picture of the logical structure of the world (*Logischer Aufbau der Welt*) as a function of the language of science *only*. Other modes of expression have only emotive meaning, or imperative. They do not give us true or false descriptions of *any* world. This has been called "scientism," though it is a more sophisticated and less offensive sort than the popular critics realize. For example, the logical positivist would reject as rank nonsense the remark that only matter is ultimately real. Such talk has no place in science proper, or anywhere else, according to logical positivism.

Then there is Wittgenstein who, like Cassirer and the earlier German idealists, gives us a more humanistic account of the language we live and think by, though in a more detailed or less systematic way. This has infuriated Russell who is more inclined toward scientism. Some of the theorists under Wittgenstein's influence have been accused by their positivistic or scientistic associates of having a leg even in existentialism (Hare). That is how informal or mercurial Wittgenstein's enigmatic pronouncements are. I am speaking of course of the maturer Wittgenstein who, when he became a man, put away the childish things he said earlier as a logical atomist, positivistically inclined. Very few of his critics have got the full significance of this awakening out of his earlier dogmatic slumber, and no philosopher has ever been as subtly imaginative and suggestive in any such awakening, not even Kant whom Hume jolted out of his dogmatic slumber. But Wittgenstein is partly to blame for the misunderstanding, perhaps even for the trivialities that some of his own disciples have spawned in his name. To prevent that—if it's worth preventing—he should have told them more systematically what he meant. But it is possible that he would not have got across as much of what he meant as he actually did communicate, if he had been more explicit.

Just two samples, in conclusion, of the sorts of things that Wittgenstein did say. He had a situational, almost organic conception of language. The terms of the language come to life, as he loved to say, in various live and working connections with one another, *and* with the situation of their use. Thus there are families or clusters of phrases that go together in the living language, and that become limp, or meaningless and perplexing, when their organic connections are broken. This happens when they are put into combinations in which their informal logic does not allow them to survive. Their animation, which is their meaning, then departs from the words, like the *anima* or the breath from a dying body, leaving it inanimate—a mere "physical object."

But let me now give you the promised examples. Suppose I say, like Descartes, that I could, while lecturing in class, be asleep and only dreaming that I am lecturing. This seems at least to be meaningful, and its truth to be an abstract possibility. But notice that the term "dreaming" has live and working connections with "awakening" and "able to report the dream upon awakening." It also ties in closely with nonverbal aspects of the situation of its use. A student might significantly think that I am sleepwalking or sleep-standing here before him, and that I am sleep-talking, if there were something eerie about my manner of speaking, and my movements somewhat mechanical or abstract, like those of the principal actor—*shite*—in a Japanese Noh play who impersonates a dead man that has temporarily come halfway out of the total inanimation of death to convey an urgent message. But is the situation like that in my daily classroom lectures? If not, then the phrase, "Maybe Aldrich is dreaming," has no working connection with the situation and so is not in use—it has no assertive force—despite appearances. It is such "appearances" that the new philosophers of the language we live by are taking stock of, in what Austin has called the phenomenology of language.

As for my own pronouncements about the state I am in, the informal logic governing the use of "dreaming" makes it *logically* impossible for me to say to someone that I am asleep and dreaming, and to *mean* it. I can say *and mean* that I am awake, but not that I am asleep and dreaming. If I am lying on a couch and you ask me if I am sleeping, my answering "Yes" could at best be a joke. Moreover, since our dreams are couched in, textured by, unspoken language, and since our "dreaming" goes with "can tell the dream," the concept of dreaming as applied, say, to a dog becomes problematic.

What Descartes did with the term "dreaming" was to cut it loose from all such connections that keep it alive with meaning, or on which its real use depends, this use being the meaning. Thus he was, unconsciously, simply toying with the term and intrigued by the imagery of what it is to be awake or dreaming that language conjures up when it "idles" in this way, tempting one to mistake these images for the meaning of the term or phrase and thus to suppose that some weird and intractable possibility forever confronts us.

These are relatively trivial examples of what the new phenomenologists of language are doing. But they do illustrate the procedure in current philosophical investigations of the language of science, morals, art, and religion, where the findings are more important. Sometimes the moral to be made about the important cases is more clearly seen, at first, in the trivial.

I said that Descartes was "unconsciously" just toying with the term "dreaming." This gets us back to the theme of my essay. Well, the present and new notion of the self and self-consciousness, philosophically construed, might be described as sensitivity to the logic of language which is our form of life since it institutes the self with its practices, including what I like to call "plain talk" *and* the more sophisticated or special languages of science, religion, etc., *and* their relations to one another. I say "sensitivity to" instead of "concept of" because such consciousness of our life-situation, including the *modus operandi* of the language we live by, is more of a *feel* for it, a watching and a hearing it at work, than a concept of it to be defined. This is one reason why Wittgenstein talked suggestively and sometimes enigmatically about our language as our soul or our form of life, instead of framing conceptually clear arguments in support of this situational theory of meaning. I conclude, then, that the self that lacks this sort of sense and sensibility has, by current standards, not realized itself. It is not self-conscious in the required way.

THE NEW IN ART

by Van Meter Ames

The new in art is becoming so new and coming so fast that it is hard even to report it, and harder to stop and appreciate or criticize it. Looking for a basis for assessment, one may wonder which of the traditional philosophies of art is most helpful or whether a fresh one is needed now. There is a parallel between novelty in art and the accelerating changes in society, owing largely to developments in science and technology. John Dewey comes to mind as foremost in advocating a reconstruction of outlook to overcome the split in our society between the advance of science, altering all practical activity, and the lag of culture, including attitudes toward art. His *Art as Experience* (1934) called for restoring the continuity between art and life. Heeding this call, or feeling it without needing to hear it, goes far to explain what is happening in the arts today and the quickening response to them.

Relating art to life might suggest that, as things in general become mechanized and routinized, art should too. But Dewey counted on science to help men live more freely and humanly, once the dislocations and aberrations of the industrial revolution were understood and corrected by the acumen which science uses and sharpens. He also saw science and art teaming up in the use of imagination and critical intelligence to recover the zest of living which, with luck and health, is natural for man as for any "live creature in the environment." Though neither artist nor scientist may think of "doing good" while doing his work, this does not reduce what he does for the common good. As the difference between art and the uses of science dwindles, so does that between fine art and other arts or ways of making. Dams, hydroelectric plants, automobiles and airplanes, launching pads and space machines all take imagination and catch it aesthetically. The satisfaction in imaginatively making needed things flows over into making things for fun, to see what can be made and what will come of it, by chance as well as by design, not only in the drips and blots of glazing and painting but in the surprises of welding and wiring, and working in the opening domain of sound. Welcoming what enters unforeseen into work, to merge with what is controlled, makes a further bond between the artist and the scientist who, with all his calculation, must at least provisionally accept the indeterminate. Peirce is confirmed in recognizing both chance and necessity in the universe. But, if he was right about a general movement from less order toward more, the artist enjoys both a more and a less predictable kind of organization.

Dewey was ahead of his time in relating art and science with life. Still, what he was able to say thirty years ago can be supplemented, as by Victorino Tejera in *Art and Human Intelligence* (1965). He takes up post-Dewey contributions to aesthetics, to show how they support him or come short of his insight that creativity in art is that of being human. Dewey's objection to the reductive fallacy in psychoanalysis holds good, that a work of art is not explained aesthetically by factors "that may—or may not—have played a part in the causative generation" of it.[1] Tejera observes: "In making the point that art excites before it is 'understood,' psychoanalysis is, after all, confirming the pragmatistic emphasis on the pre-reflective phase of any experiential situation . . ." And Merleau-Ponty is like Dewey in relating aesthetics to "the phases of life-situations."[2] Eugene Kaelin had already associated Dewey with Merleau-Ponty in saying that, for existentialist and pragmatist alike, "what is being deplored is the separation of art experiences from the ordinary experiences which make up the lives of men." Also: "It is significant that Merleau-Ponty, like Dewey, may be said to have begun his aesthetics with an account of 'the live creature.' "[3]

Not only philosophers but nearly everyone discussing art recently brings out the connection with life and the state of society. The connection is often seen to be a tension between art and the public, or between the creativity of art and much that passes for art. Thirty years ago Dewey asked: "Why is the architecture of our large cities so unworthy of a fine civilization? . . . not merely slums but the apartments of the well-to-do . . . are so destitute of imagination. Their character is determined by an economic system . . ."[4] Adorno sees the serious composer now, and the musician who would perform his work, in conflict with the "culture industry."[5] Even in jazz the popular demand prevents performers, who must earn a living, from doing what for them is the real thing.[6] George Amberg feels obliged to say that "proportionately with the increase of the audience diminishes the value of its aesthetic appreciation." And: ". . . the mass media threaten to create an imbalance between artistic supply and demand that can only be stabilized by increasing production at the expense of quality."[7]

Since there is justification for such pessimism, the effort to create today involves the urge to rebel, at the risk of imitating gestures that were fresh when dada and surrealism defied society in the 1920's and 1930's. The push to free the human spirit from inertia and reaction will be carried on by art worthy of the name, even if unworthy absurdities are repeated. Sartre spotted the contradiction between the surrender of the mind in the "automatic" productions of the surrealists and their assertion of individual and social responsibility. But, if Sartre is right about their "flickering" between incompatible positions and counting on a magic of chance to produce unity, Roger Shattuck thinks: "'Flickering' is not at all a bad word to describe . . . registering a wide range of experience . . . in communication with other minds or forces." It is appealing that, unlike their successors the existentialists, the surrealists were not anguished but delighted by "the bizarre inconsistencies of life," without ceasing to criticize society.[8] If it is time to move on, it would be good to recover their idealism and see that, under the fun and fooling, to be an artist is not to be a freak but a person.

To think the zest of making and enjoying art is only for a few is to fear that some of the best of life cannot be made available to everyone. So many things now are made readily available, ready to wear, ready to eat or heat, it may seem that art too should be mass-produced if not pre-appreciated. If everyone should be free to read the best books, at least these should be printed copiously and economically enough to be within easy reach. And people should be free to make up their own minds about books in doubt. But this requires the ability and the will, which cannot be taken for granted, to read with the mind's eye open and not just feed on print. There is no escaping the need for more and better education. Painting and sculpture are brought to the public in permanent and traveling exhibitions. There are "artmobiles" as well as "bookmobiles." But people must learn what it can mean to look. Reproductions have become cheap enough to have at home. Records and tapes of music have increased interest even in much that is far from popular. If it is important to compare reproductions of visual art with the originals, it is easier now for crowds to travel and see for themselves. If accessibility and familiarity develop immunity to the established things of beauty, and even prevent the effort to enjoy newer works, apparently night clubs and sports, if not circuses, will continue to entertain for nothing but money. But pastimes, to be more rewarding than boring for people who know the difference, require participation in the effort and skill that approach art or become indistinguishable from it. If Duchamp has been assiduous at chess he did not altogether give up art. And no matter how numerous the knowing and doing few become who really care about art, or how much they learn, there is always more to try. What is being done maintains a frontier.

It is easy to deride the idea that more than a minority will ever be discriminating, and to ridicule the effort to spread art education in schools and colleges. All education has faults enough to make an easy mark. But the proposal to educate everyone is so recent, and the problem of educating anyone so complicated, that the headway already made should be encouraging. What has been achieved in awakening interest and latent talent in children is amazing, in painting, music, and other arts where the attempt has been resourceful. Classes for adults have also been worth while. What if the number of geniuses is limited? Whitman said, "To have great art there must be great audiences." But why care how much is great? There has been too much acceptance of the misguided spirit of commercialized sport, exaggerating competitiveness to the point where it seems a waste of time to play and not win, not be the best, the greatest. Especially in art this makes no sense, where individuality counts so much as to make grading irrelevant if not impossible. A city, instead of enjoying its orchestra for what it does, and wanting it to do *its* best, wants it rated above rivals. If conductors can be compared, their differences cannot. Umpires and scorekeepers are not necessary for a game. Art does not exist for the sake of critics, and certainly not when they would be judges. As the playing is the thing, so is the painting, the writing, the building, the making of any kind. That is enough for the maker, or for the appreciator who is *with* him. Who gets left may laugh, or try to catch on.

What to make of what is made leads to questions which may affect and even help what is being done. But criticism which counts must be so close to making as to be like the eye that does not guide the hand so much as follow what the hand does, it knows not how but feels. Since art for Dewey draws its force from close to the source of life, criticism is important less in finding fault, and still less in giving grades, than in perceiving the unique vitalizing qualities of a work and opening eyes to them. This requires knowing what artists have done before, while keeping up with what they are up to. Dewey realizes that the artist, though feeling his way or plunging on without stopping to think, also uses thinking as strenuous as that of the scientist. Thought for both is, to begin with and again to go on with, hunches and patches, but piecing them together and sighting ahead to calculate their drift is an intellectual process. If the work of the scientist is for the sake of what can be done with it, more than for appreciation of what it is in itself, the main use of science is for further science, whatever the uses along the way, however practical or earthshaking. So too, the work of the artist leads to more art, which turns out to be further work in progress, for him or for others. Art and science belong to the full career of the live creature when he becomes human enough to be creative, solving problems only to set up or get into more, which are the breath of life as long as he can cope with them.

Part of the interest in art is in the fresh experience it provides or brings to light. The other part is in the technical means employed. Human experience always has been and is increasingly inseparable from the means, the tools and devices used. These may at first be intended simply to improve previous methods, to facilitate the familiar ways of making the same things, doing the same chores, going about the old roads, fighting the old battles. But inevitably, doing things differently leads to doing different things. New kinds of work and play and war keep changing the way people live and feel, and how they think. All this is reflected, abetted and accelerated in art. New art forms make use of antecedent and even rather new technologies. Marshall McLuhan sees that the industrial (mechanical) revolution put what had been "nature" into art, and that electric technology made its mechanical predecessor into the content and form of art for "futurists, cubists, Vorticists, and others." Pop art uses "the old environment of advertising technology. . . . When the film was new, it used the novel and drama as content . . . in the documentary, it was in effect using the newspaper as content. Dickens anticipated the form of film when he was most documentary. . . . D. W. Griffiths . . . habitually carried a volume of Dickens with him on location."[9]

The fascination of the film for all kinds of people has been its power to present unlimited aspects of the world realistically. But sticking to reality, asking things and persons just to speak for themselves, as if that sufficed for art, often has resulted in the flat and lifeless. Yet departure from the expected naturalism is not easily accepted, as in the conventions of the theater. A Naples scene must seem to be in Naples and not in Paris. Not only settings and furnishings are enjoyed for their faithfulness to reality. Actors are admired for their own physical and personal charms rather than for ability to impersonate characters. As Professor Bianca has also pointed out, in television especially, the sense of immediacy and spontaneity, the seeming to be present at what is just occurring, even though it was filmed some time before, counts above all. For Bianca this answers to "a religious need to see and hear, in the world we live in, a resonance and extension of our own psychic states," to reassure us that we are not alone in an indifferent universe.[10]

Comic films amuse by getting away from reality, though not too far, as they frolic on well-worn tracks. Films in general, for all their realism, have accustomed the public to tricks of montage which scramble space and time, as in the novels of Proust and Joyce. Arnold Hauser said that the film "has made it possible to represent visually experiences that have previously been expressed only in musical forms." When, however, he said that "the film is not finding its writers or . . . the writers are not finding their way to the film," he did not know that Robbe-Grillet would write for *Last Year at Marienbad,* or Marguerite Duras for *Hiroshima Mon Amour*. Hauser did know that Eisenstein and other Russians had developed a method of "short cutting" which gave "speed and rhythm" to "the change of shots" and extended "the boundaries of the cinematically feasible." Still, it struck Hauser that the "revolutionary quality of this montage technique" was less important than "the fact that it was no longer the phenomena of a homogeneous world of objects, but of quite heterogeneous elements of reality, that were brought face to face." Coming from Italy lately, the discontinuities, irrelevancies, strange double exposures of scenes as different as baths and launching pads, beds and cars, with a director filmed in search of his film and cast, in Federico Fellini's *8½*, are difficult for people not initiated in the discrepancies and non sequiturs of happenings in other arts. As movie tricks become familiar, people lose interest in them and want back the "well told story" or the fact and actuality of the "document," though Hauser agrees with Bianca that this means "very often a renunciation of art altogether."[11] But the "art movie" does not have to avoid reality when it can fit fancy to fact. The imaginative need not be imaginary.

In painting, the relation to reality has become complicated. Alan Solomon, who organized the two American exhibitions at the Biennale XXXII, stresses the involvement of the viewer "directly in the artist's struggle with his problem" in the "arena" of the canvas. Whether reference to "the real world" is avoided, or familiar objects are translated to a new reality, the chief interest is in the dynamic tension of the artist's very real activity. There is the exciting way the late Morris Louis achieved his "veils" with "an effect of chromatic translucency . . . by tacking the unstretched canvas on a slanting frame and flooding thin washes . . . onto the surface at the top, directly from the can." Staple holes show how, in a happy combination of skill and luck, he gathered and fastened folds in the canvas "to provide channels to control the flow of the paint. . . . Since the paintings never had a chance to dry as he worked, it is difficult to imagine how he kept the rows of color so close without having them fuse . . ." The tension in Jasper Johns is different. In his flag painting he forces a new look at the commonplace, and yet "he retains the animated, worked surface of abstract expressionism; like Rauschenberg, he uses it as a foil to introduce an element of ambiguity between the real and the painted. . . . His irony rests on the fact that his paintings remain rich and . . . limitlessly evocative, *in spite of* their violations of all our preconceptions."[12]

In Venice there was the open question of American pop art. Remote origin, history or poetry can do wonders with ordinary things. Household utensils dug up by archaeologists have the glory of Greece as well as their form to thank for being admired as art. The Pylos bathtub, celebrated by Homer, would be aesthetic even if not marble. But Homer honored things of use because they had the honor of being used, whether ship, shield, or tub. If things we use must go unsung, we are unwilling to be ourselves. Pop art faces us with what we make and live with, by daring to dispense with aesthetic distance and by providing it surprisingly, so that we have to stop and consider instead of just buying, using, or passing by. Things may be shiny-new as Jim Dine's "Shovel" or battered as the bucket, rickety as the ladder, worn as the bed quilt in the "combines" of Rauschenberg when he won the first prize in the Biennale XXXII in 1964. John Chamberlain exploited "the inherent formal qualities, the curvilinear energy, and the expressive roughness and tactility of scrap automobile parts."[13] Claes Oldenburg mimicked and magnified consumer articles. Pop artists force realization that cities and technology have become our "nature." We must accept a bathroom rather than a sylvan dale as the scene of bathing. Suddenly we are made to see who we are when it startles us to look for art and see our plumbing fixtures, the elements of our billboards and comic strips, the appearance of our women now, the way beer is canned and labeled, and sandwiches decked. Here, in terms of today, are the elemental things of religion and original art. Here are food, drink, sex, and ablution now. Dewey expected art to clarify life. The artist is not to blame when his clarity is hard on us.

Dewey is more than confirmed in his conviction that almost anything can provide content and suggest form for art. He observed that railway coaches, "actually third class," appealed to Daumier, "apples, napkins, and plates" to Cézanne. What counted was not these things but what was done with them. Cézanne was not "doing" his wife but a painting never meant to do her justice as a portrait when she sat for him. In the 1964 international art shows of the Biennale at Venice and the Documenta III at Kassel, there was much that did not take off from anything as long familiar as railway coaches, dishes or women, but from mad mechanisms or from experiments with shifting colored light. Still, Dewey was apropos in saying: "Art throws off the covers that hide the expressiveness of experienced things . . . and orders them in a new experience of life."[14] Jean Dubuffet, in his painting and lithography at the Biennale, had series and suites of the components of earth, of ocean, of sand under water, the splash of sun and shade, the texture of skin, of dust, of vegetation. Returning to the human scene, he plunged into the crowd to make colored patterns of intricate streets, flat and twisted autos and people, gay as peppermint sticks. Instead of simply taking over, he made over. Even when he kept to what was under foot, in soil or pavement, there was his own making, as he transferred what he saw to what he did with a medium.

Dewey spoke for many a painter in saying: "Any product whose quality is not of the very 'easy' sort exhibits dislocations. . . . Ordinary prepossession must be broken through if the degree of energy required for an esthetic experience is to be evoked."[15] Yet he did not take sufficient account of art that is very difficult to enjoy. He assumed that even unlovely art should be exhilarating. Roberto E. Matta had a triptych in Kassel, showing an anxious couple pushed aside by a technology out of control. Yet here was Dewey's theme that, because "science has brought with it a radically novel conception of physical nature and of our relation to it . . . things of the physical world and those of the moral realm have fallen apart

. . ."[16] The dire consequence of such disruption was evident in the canvases of Fritz Winter, painted in hiding from the Nazis—dark, complex—and in monstrous, lumpy human shapes in bronze by Otto Freundlich. "Frankfurter Frühling" by Otto-Herbert Hajek was done in "elements" of concrete and color like the wreck of a building. In Venice, Giovanni Paganin's bronze "Adamo" and "Madre" stood hacked and blasted beyond a trace of grace. Pierluca's "Grande Lacerazione," in aluminum, was a gaping gash. Here was more than the "not easy" that Dewey allowed for, although he could have known Goya's "Massacre of the Citizens of Madrid," Edvard Munch's "The Scream," and the work of Käthe Kollwitz.

Ivan Albright of Chicago does not show the catastrophic effects of science or war but only what happens anyway, in a manner devastating to a comfortable view: the aging of human flesh, the dust on all we have. Dubuffet expressed his own admiration for Albright's revelation of a "crumbling . . . world . . . in place of the one in which we had believed we lived . . . constituted of objects thrown into a terrifying isolation . . . unchained disorder." Yet Dubuffet felt that, if we can do without "the tranquillity obtained by means of blindness" and "opt for navigation in the great deeps," we will not want his work burned.[17] Nor if we have some of Albright's sympathy for the way of flesh and the wear on things we live with. We may enjoy his mastery of paint itself, as we do the inventive control of the medium by other disquieting artists. When we become more seeing and more impatient with ugliness we also come to wonder whether anything is intrinsically ugly or beyond the wand of transformation, any more than in the fairy tale of Beauty and the Beast. But in the "literary" or social implications of art, inseparable from the technical side, whether intended or not, we cannot escape indictment of a society which has not done what it could to alleviate the human condition, fateful as it must remain.

Since most art education has been traditional, people who have been taught what art is cannot quickly discard invidious distinction between "fine art" and lesser art (or less than art), to admire or accept the departures appearing now as the work of artists. There are the changing hues and luminosities, on revolving forms, shining through glass. Findings of the laboratory, the clack and clank of shop and factory reveal their own possibilities of fascination. Multiple reflections of balls on strings, easy to jiggle, tiny white disks trembling on spring-like stems when breathed on, compete with arrangements to give only the illusion of motion. The artist cannot be satisfied to copy or repeat the work of the past. He must be impatient if not contemptuous toward people content with hand-me-down notions of subject matter and pleased with hackneyed techniques. It is surprising when he sells or suits the box office. He would agree with Dewey's saying: "What happens in the movement of art is emergence of new materials of experience demanding expression, and therefore involving . . . new forms and techniques."[18]

Not to be ignored is the growing number of people, with no interest in "fine art," who have lived in touch with shops, factories, and garages, if not in them or in what Peirce called "the laboratory band," used to having tools in their hands, even power tools, and enthusiastic about what can be done with them, not just to get work done but for fun. They have a fellow feeling for the makers of newfangled contrivances under the heading of *Licht und Bewegung* in Documenta III or included in *Arte d'Oggi* in Biennale XXXII. Gillo Dorfles said of the Biennale that the artisan's technical control largely accounted for the things on display. He asked whether Rauschenberg had ever been surpassed in using real objects to reveal an aesthetic-social atmosphere while successfully working them into painting. Dorfles admitted the crudity of Oldenburg's and Chamberlain's productions, but welcomed the "osmosis between the art of the élite and the art of the masses," and concluded that "neither social nor technical problems can be ignored in this day and age."[19]

Art obliges us to take a fresh look around us. A change comes over an object from a wrecked car lot merely in being exhibited, lighted, seen from a new angle, put on a pedestal: a ruined radiator or a broken axle. It is just a step from the junk object to junk sculpture, as from a found object to a constructed one. When what had been thought to be a work of art is "proved to be an accidental natural product," Dewey said, it is reduced from art to "a natural 'curiosity.' " For him, "making" or its absence made that much difference. This is difficult to accept when aesthetic interest is taken in driftwood, in shells and stones, partly or largely because they are not art objects but "just as good," not to mention the spacious "beauties of nature." A merely found object is impregnated with aesthetic value when its constitutive trail of events includes having been selected and kept as if made, while admired for not being man-made. To regard something as if it were art is at least on the way to making it art, since a real part of any art is seeing what is already given in the material. Ordinarily the material needs to be worked up into a medium, and the medium worked into something further, but the amount of work and reworking is always more or less. Why not say work is reduced to a minimum when all that has to be done is to delight in what is found? This question may be rhetorical, as shown in the book by Gyorgy Kepes illustrating "The New Landscape Exhibition" at M.I.T. in 1951, where scientists' photographs not intended as art can be mistaken for artists' paintings.[20]

There is no doubt about advance in science and technology. Whether it is possible to paint better than the cave artists of Lascaux or to write better than Isaiah or Tu Fu, if there is no room for improvement, there is room for difference. The development of reflective or critical ability, when it becomes more analytical and mathematical, leads to programming a series of steps to follow automatically. Losing the liberty to introduce further moves of his own, the artist may seek to recover his freedom from the grip of number by relying entirely on chance and accident. But this is another way of tying his mind behind his back. Extremes of calculation and the aleatory both reduce the artist to a helpless spectator of work slipping out of his control. Effort to avoid effort becomes self-defeating for an artist, because he ceases to be one if he long foregoes the constant touch and adjustment of being alive to a live situation, like an alert sailor in rough weather, or anyone who has to keep his wits about him. Not to need vigilance, resource and sagacity, with imagination, is not to be really living as a human being, and certainly not as an artist, though luck will count. While an artist needs to use his head, he will agree with Dewey that "the unexpected turn, something which the artist himself does not definitely foresee, is a condition of the felicitous quality of a work of art . . ."[21]

There is a tantalizing question as to how skill and luck come together. Each seems to bring out the other. Strokes of genius come to a genius as star performance to a born athlete. The artist adroitly turns to advantage what turns up. He will shape his carving to the grain or knots in wood, the veins in marble. He will use the way the paint runs, the glaze drips. He will go along as well as take charge. When well mounted he will hold a loose rein, as a good rider will do when he can. As horse and rider become one, so do work and worker. In the rhythm of the organism the hand shows the head as much as the head tells the hand, or more. Victorino Tejera says: "The 'rightness' of works of art is based on their congruence with human sensory processes, not on systematic consistency like the theoretical products of intelligence."[22]

This was confirmed by the composers and devotees of new music in the summer gatherings at Darmstadt. In 1952 they had their first presentation of electronic music. In 1957 music from India was demonstrated in its endless variation and improvisation, within the bounds of tradition. Also in 1957 Karlheinz Stockhausen's "Klavierstück XI" showed that he had moved from his previous idea, that electronic tapes would replace performers, to the principle of inexhaustible variation and interpretation. In the same season Pierre Boulez gave his lecture on "Alea," which he illustrated by playing his "Third Piano Sonata," explaining the mistake of contriving a scheme to take over a piece completely.[23]

This mistake has to be watched in other arts where mathematical precision or programming is also tried. There is the "use of modules in architecture, the word-counts and 'text-algebra' applied to poetry . . . the whole notion of 'permutational art' . . . a new and would-be exact formalism." There is also a spreading endeavor to fuse the permutational-precisionist method with the artist's freedom to go on making decisions and taking advantage of accidents. Since we are acquiring new instruments, "we may as well learn how to play them as we already play the typewriter, the printing press, the symphony orchestra, the film studio and other pieces of apparatus." One may write poetry with a computer, but to rely too much on its permutations may have a result as tedious and senseless as trusting to the "automatisms" of the subconscious. Work with words in purely verbal patterns becomes a highly conscious reduction of language to its own terms, with no reference to anything but words, much as Kandinsky freed painting from objects. The consequent obscurity in Max Bense and his Stuttgart group, and in similar groups of new writers in other countries, goes with an intellectual elegance which admittedly shuts out appalling things that words would evoke if allowed to stray off the page. These people have found a way of writing when there is nothing to say. Refraining from saying makes a close relation between their technical and their social motivation.[24]

In music it is easier to avoid reference to events, though social protest may enter in more than might be supposed. But in composing music, as in writing poetry, there is the same question today of how much to rely upon the exact formalism of new permutational methods. The conclusion of Boulez comes to uniting the irrational with the rational, to keep surprise, which means to him that not only the composer but the performer must be free to make decisions. Still, Boulez wants to keep a feeling of necessity,[25] whereas his friend and colleague John Cage wants to get away from any sense of necessity as much as possible. And Cage feels as free with tapes as with conventional instruments, delighting in the opening up of the whole field of sound by the new devices. Yet, eager as he is to let sounds be themselves, it is clear that he is busy organizing them in various ways instead of just letting them happen. Having studied with Schoenberg, and knowing what there is to know about music, Cage not only invites chance but is skillful with it.[26] But artists, like other men, often seem afraid of freedom as soon as they attain it. Strangely, they clamp it down again with imposed order, even when they have learned that no conventions are binding or lasting. Cage appears to many as an *enfant terrible* because he seeks in his music (and in his writing) as much discontinuity as he can get in a composition. He does not mind form if it is loose enough. Boulez wants spontaneity if it is controlled enough. Between them they personify the bipolar tension in contemporary art.

In architecture, utilitarian and durable though it usually must be, accident and plan come together as in music. Differences of climate, difficulties of topography, what there is to build with, and what has to be housed enter in. The idea that architecture is "frozen music" has melted. Bernard Rudofsky has shown: "There is much to learn from architecture before it became an expert's art." His illustrations in *Architecture Without Architects* make a modern Western reader wonder how his society could give up so much imagination.[27] Now there is American appreciation of surprise in the city planning of Europe. Esther McCoy speaks of "the delight of turning a corner of an Italian street and coming unexpectedly upon a fountain, a courtyard or an exciting perspective."[28] The architect John M. Johansen is interested "in processes rather than finality; improvisation rather than predetermination." He says: "Because it is difficult today to anticipate the future uses of a building, producing precious and exquisite designs is folly. The idea of growth should not only be a part of planning, but a part of aesthetics as well." He is "willing to allow the half-designed building to assert its own young will. . . . Elements of a kind, or elements unlike, grow together, accumulate, build up by natural process . . . mechanical equipment, like vents, and exhaust housing tunnels" make their contribution openly to the visible structure, along with "boxes for rooms, tubes for corridors, towers for stairs."[29]

This is like letting everyday sounds into music, or ordinary objects into the "combines" of Rauschenberg. So modern dance, notably in the work of Martha Graham and Merce Cunningham, as Cage has said, will "introduce an audience, not to a specialized world of art, but to the open, unpredictably changing, world of everyday living."[30] Much the same can be said of the theater today, when it is of today, as of photography and the movies. Here is the spirit of Wordsworth, going from "poetic" diction down to the idiom of common life and speech; also the spirit of Whitman, Pound, and on to Robert Lowell and John Berryman. William Carlos Williams is belatedly appreciated for working out his way of voicing love for ordinary things and fellow beings, a river, a person, a sparrow, or buds on a branch. He joined Duchamp in presenting unmodified "objects," though also learning to work in their worth. As Thom Gunn has seen, Williams "insisted on the American idiom" in the belief that writing "thoroughly local in origin has some chance of being universal in application."[31] In the foreword to the Fiftieth Anniversary issue of *Poetry,* the editor Henry Rago wrote: "Mr. Pound's *Make It New* will not be eluded—what is good is what is new. There is no point otherwise in writing the poem. A poet does not write the poem he knows can be written; he writes what he will know only when he has written it. . . . The good poem is always a surprise."[32]

In John Berryman the new is so irreverent toward tradition, so highwrought that the reader cannot sit back and be lulled or soothed, but is jostled awake. He has to pay attention, watch for irony, use all he knows and feels, fears and doubts, as well as hopes. To freshen speech, clichés are rejected or used brutally, syntax is broken, English departments are spoofed. The crack of the vernacular is heard, the retort and repartee of vaudeville, of night spots and garages, family circles. There is no filling or coasting. Anything is used, out of the paper or out of the past, to play with or depart from, unless it cannot be said better. Then it is allowed to stand and speak for itself, and for us. Dewey seems to have meant this when he said that art aims at "a full and intense experience," and so "keeps alive the power to experience the common world in its fullness."[33]

The simple trajectory is out of favor in verbal work as in music. The rational linear form of before and after becomes multidimensional. Not only is a straightforward sequence of narration or ideation jumbled up. A sentence may not admit of being parsed. Even the familiar relationship of letters in a word may be disordered, as in Joyce's punning and playing hob with English, though the fun must depend upon still knowing what is departed from. If Joyce's Irish resentment against having to use the language of England was involved, this is further evidence of the close relation between social and artistic creation and criticism. But, without Joyce's vast knowledge, intelligence, and patience, it is possible now to carry on in his wake with no serious or very personal effort of imagination. Irreverent antics, though almost automatic, elicit a response from readiness to rebel against a self-righteously superior culture which has mantled itself with an air of rationality.

More than other artists, writers are expected to react to the social situation, but with the help of the others in developing new techniques. Michel Butor, returning the compliment of Pierre Boulez, admits the influence not only of Pound, Joyce, and French literary explorers, but also of the new composers. Butor has collaborated with the Belgian composer Henri Pousseur in a treatment of the Faust theme, in which only some of the musical choices are used in any one performance.[34] One way of introducing the unpredictable is now and then to draw someone at random from the audience on to the stage. In Butor's novel *L'Emploi du Temps,* the map of a city is like a score which can be taken up at any point in any direction. Plunging in and wandering at will is invited in Butor's *Mobile,* as in Joyce's complex constructions. With the typographical experiments of Rabelais and Mallarmé in mind, Butor has used some of the new procedures in printing technology for overcoming the linear monotony of the page.[35]

Cage and Boulez exemplify the freemasonry among the various arts today. Cage began with poetry and went on to architecture before studying with Schoenberg. Boulez, influenced by the novels of Joyce, Kafka, Butor, and the poetry of Mallarmé (who used musical models), wanted to compose in a way to escape "a simple trajectory, traced between a point of departure and a point of arrival," which practically eliminates surprise.[36] And Boulez likes Henry Miller's saying that accident contributes to a masterwork. Mistakes, backtracking and corrections help inspiration.[37]

As influential as James Joyce upon recent fiction is Franz Kafka. His K characters are not persons in particular but any reflective individuals who feel threatened by nearly everything in the impersonal modern world. Now that the self is felt to be in jeopardy, the highly individual expression of Mallarmé, Rilke, and Emily Dickinson is a defense and a comfort. So is the older "poetry of sensibility," as Kenneth Rexroth calls it, in his versions from the Chinese, the Japanese, and the Greek.[38] The impossibility of living apart makes tension between the self and others, a yearning to get away, and so for criticism of society along with the song of fellow feeling. The violent reaction of Poe, Baudelaire, and Rimbaud against their time and place drove their poetry away; but their estrangement has become only too common, in spite of the sense that, deep down, no self is separate.

The *nouveau roman* practically does without characters and the plots that went with them. Samuel Beckett & Co. represent what Wylie Sypher has called, in the title of his book, *Loss of the Self in Modern Literature and Art.* Sypher goes back to Gide's principle of the discontinuity of the self, shared with Dostoevsky. Conrad is seen "able to dismantle the Western self" in *The Heart of Darkness.* Robert Musil's hero without qualities, in *Der Mann Ohne Eigenschaften,* was made to order for Sypher. If he is convincing, then it is desperate for Sartre and the literary existentialists to hold on to the self, disillusioned and precarious as it is for them, in a world of not-self and of other selves bent on reducing one's own self to an object. Sypher recalls that Hamlet and Julien Sorel had doubts about the self, and finds the anti-novel's denial of a continuous or solid self in Hardy's *Jude the Obscure;* also in Sterne's *Tristram Shandy;* further, in drama from Strindberg to Ionesco. Sypher concludes that Hiroshima and the concentration camps ruined the "Promethean image of man."[39]

No one can say it has not been shaken. But in speaking of "the scuttling of literature" when "Verlaine wanted to take eloquence and wring its neck," or when Lewis Carroll wrote "anti-poetry," Sypher forgets the denial in his foreword that he is "attacking modern art." He calls the "anti-painting" of the impressionists "the ruination of art," and deplores "the subversion of art now in progress." To take Dubuffet's word that his painting is "anti-painting" and repeat his shouting "Down with galleries! Down with museums! Down with art critics and dealers!" as if this announced the end of painting instead of trumpeting a summons to make it new, is to miss the message. Sypher proceeds to equate Dubuffet's readiness to paint anything, and his having no "compulsion to choose," with Zen capacity to "feel a unity between the self and things," and then asserts that in both Dubuffet and Zen the refusal to be choosy is a "brutal" sacrifice of the self. Only by identifying loss of self with loss of the self-centered Romantic conception of self could the zest of Zen and the exhilaration of Dubuffet be thought to sacrifice anything. Sypher himself corrects this in saying that when Dubuffet "has absorbed the painter in his painting" he is "losing nothing."[40] All that is lost is separateness, which is an illusion. John Cage clarifies the point in writing: "It is not a question of going in to oneself or out to the world. It is rather a condition of fluency that's in and out." And: ". . . one must see that humanity and nature, not separate, are in this world together, that nothing was lost when everything was given away." Zen does not abandon the self or anything to an absolute, but sees things as they are, in themselves as well as in relations and in the whole. Cage heard Suzuki say: ". . . in all space each thing and each human being is at the center and furthermore . . . each one being at the center is the most honored of all. Interpenetration means that each one of these most honored ones of all is moving out in all directions."[41]

So with Dubuffet. So with Cage. Neither Cage nor dancer Merce Cunningham, nor painter Robert Rauschenberg, nor pianist David Tudor lost a thing, let alone a self, when they evolved together a combination of movement, sight and sound that won acclaim across the Atlantic and the Pacific as well as in New York. Applause and renown are not necessary to a self, even for an artist. It can be enough for him to have his work and "give himself" to it, when it enables him to make his own decisions and his own difference. For others, interest in his life may displace interest in his *oeuvre,* with the justification that to think finished work is what makes the maker an artist is to put the cart before the horse. It puts matters back in their right order to see the artist as a man making, ahead of what he makes, not to mention his preceding the appreciator, the collector, the curator, and the critic. Making might seem to be in vain without their looking. But the artist makes them possible, and he can do without them. Growing interest in the activity of the artist goes with realization that here, as in science, but more in view and closer home, is evolution coming alive in the acts of men, becoming little by little, then more and more, their venture, their doing, and their choosing.

Even in the scientists' photographs in the Kepes volume, making remained. Though not intended to be art, there was human selection in the focus of the camera. There was the edge between a picture and what was left out. We may simply have to say with Merleau-Ponty that fresh perception itself is aesthetic; and that whatever nature or man does tends to be aesthetic or artistic, if at all what a man enjoys or does when living as a healthy and untrammeled animal grown human.

Since it is now clear that life is inherently an unfinished business, that our universe itself is "in the making," as William James said, and that man is taking more part in the making, it is not surprising that the 1964 Congress on Aesthetics in Amsterdam was much taken up with the *non-finito.* Fascination with the unfinished follows the shift away from passive acceptance or admiration of art things regarded, like things in general, as naturally or miraculously there rather than as having been made, or made by remote creation—if by men, then by geniuses of another time and race, poles apart from the rest of men. Dewey occasionally seems old-fashioned when he values completeness as a trait of preferred experience, in contrast to the common dismissal, in much recent art, of any attempt to reach a terminal whole. Thinking of art not as thing but as activity, not as finished work but as ways of working, heightens interest in the creative processes of artists who may be local, whose latest undertaking is hardly dry or not yet performed. It is not felt to be definitive but in mid-career, as likely to veer as the course of a chipmunk, child, or energetic man. So De Kooning slashes with his brush, scrapes, slashes again, with no final goal.

Ezra Pound's "Make it new" holds good, but so does the old love of life. In fact, they are the same. But the artist's urge to celebrate existence turns to resentment, at least implied, against what society does or fails to do which thwarts or dulls natural delight. So the critical aspect of art is not confined to freeing it from lifeless forms. Technical and professional use of critical acumen in the artist's work is at the same time inevitably directed against social abuses and failures. Anything which keeps people from being free and creative persons will hamper and arouse them as artists. D. W. Gotshalk has well shown that art has social implications even as "a purely aesthetic enterprise," since these are "part of its artistic structure," in as much as the materials, forms, and expressions of art are those of life, focused and emphasized. "There is no need to sacrifice artistic subtlety for doctrinal explicitness. The art can become saturated with the outlook of the artist, and this outlook can be empowered by all the subtleties and devices of the art."[42] Adorno has written of the musician's revulsion against the degradation of music in radio and film, especially in the singing commercial: "The isolation of radical modern music comes not from its a-social but from its social content."[43] And Kallen: ". . . the liberty of the artist . . . has become the avatar of all the freedoms men fight and are ready to die for. It is the spontaneity and fertility of the very life of us, and so contagious that where the artist is free no other man can remain bond."[44]

The architect Johansen has said: "Mass production has not fully served human needs, and has served the psyche not at all. . . . There is skepticism about institutionalized religion, disillusionment with our society, disengagement and disenchantment among our youth." And since these attitudes are deep and widespread, "it is natural that the arts should express them."[45]

In the same vein Dewey has said that "since the surroundings which man has made, under the influence of modern industry, afford less fulfillment and more repulsion than at any previous time, there is only too evidently a problem that is still unsolved." Though "production for private gain" is much to blame, the answer is not merely in "social alteration." Men need to realize what it could mean to live with more freedom and imagination, and here is the moral function of art. Dewey held "that art is more moral than moralities. For the latter either are, or tend to become, consecrations of the *status quo,* reflections of custom, reenforcements of the established order. . . . Art has been the means of keeping alive the sense of purposes that outrun evidence and of meanings that transcend indurated habit."[46]

When many people have little interest in what they do, and little sense of really doing or deciding anything, a mood of emptiness and absurdity is general. War, overpopulation, and automation are hard on the Romantic name-self, but also on the semi-nameless one. Yet the Promethean spirit is no more chained than challenged. It is stirring to break free and make a society which will let people become persons, and help them to. The depressing "residue of selfhood" in Beckett sounds a warning. If that is what we are coming to, we are indebted to his art for jarring us awake to it.

The way back from such a dead end does not lie in exaggerating the self again, but in restoring everyday experience so that people can like what they do and where they live, privately and together. This seems to be what Dewey hoped for in recovering continuity between the fine and the useful in art and life. Much the same fusion of the unique and the usual is cherished in Suzuki's *Zen and Japanese Culture,*[47] and in Hisamatsu's *Zen and Fine Arts.*[48] In Japan as in America, however, the hope is not to return to what once made a good life but to work out what can be a good life now, in spite of or with the help of new developments. Perhaps life cannot be better than it has been for a few in the past. The need is to use the new means to improve living for more people.

This calls for more relation between art and industrialism. To a growing number of people, instead of measuring art by suitability for museum exhibition or having at home, with invitations to see and discuss painting, drawing, sculpture, and individual works in various media, there should be a shift to concern with making the environment more aesthetic. Critical aesthetic attention should be given to how transportation is designed, how printing and labeling are done in merchandising, how food is prepared and served, how housing is produced with new uses of steel, concrete, wood, plastics, membrane, and how whole neighborhoods are planned in the development of a city. Such redirection of aesthetic interest leads to tours of new dwellings and buildings; also of old sections of a city which often are newly appreciated on the eve of demolition. The result is a rekindling of civic pride, with wider and more discerning participation in decisions to restore or rebuild. Then cooperation is more possible, though conflict still threatens the long approach to a truly human community. How much art in all its forms can help toward that goal may be wondered. At least it is clear that art crosses national borders in a grand give and take of influence and response, ever trying out what can be done with what has been done, with what there is and is coming to be. It does not follow that there should be a moratorium on more personal art, since all art has a social function, especially now, urging us to change our life, with the double shove of the creative and the critical.

Much as we admire the artist as individual, we see that artists come in schools, and that the same movements pervade all the arts. Some arts have always combined the talents of committees and teams. Without cooperation there would have been no cathedrals or other architecture, no theater, no opera or ballet, no music to speak of, or film or television. City and regional planning must be collective. Often as not, it is in working together that men do their best as individuals. When they appear to work alone they have the company of colleagues and rivals, living or dead.

Offsetting the fear that men will not only be driven but bred and led to live without personality, and like it or no longer care, there is promise in the critical and creative activity of contemporary art, which joins or uses the same dual force of science. Such power is dangerous and may be disastrous, if its own controls get out of control. But man does have the capacity to see where he is heading, far enough ahead to change course while it is not too late. The future of the human race is in doubt, and that of art is bound up with it, but it is too soon to announce the ruination of art when it is being renewed all around. With such vitality in art, there is a chance for life.

NOTES

1. John Dewey, *Art As Experience* (New York, 1934), p. 316. References are to this edition. Now also in Capricorn paperback.
2. Victorino Tejera, *Art and Human Intelligence* (New York, 1965), pp. 97, 157.
3. Eugene F. Kaelin, *An Existentialist Aesthetic: The Theories of Sartre and Merleau-Ponty* (Madison, 1962), p. 341.
4. Dewey, *Art As Experience,* p. 344.
5. Cf. Theodor W. Adorno, *Einleitung in die Musiksoziologie* (Frankfurt, 1962).

6. Cf. Richard A. Peterson, "Artistic Creativity and Alienation: The Jazz Musician Vs. His Audience," *Arts in Society,* III, No. 2 (1965), 244-248.
7. George Amberg, "Pop Avant-Garde," *ibid.,* pp. 257, 261.
8. Cf. Roger Shattuck, "Love and Laughter: Surrealism Reappraised," *ibid.,* pp. 158, 159.
9. Marshall McLuhan, "The New Media and the Arts," *ibid.,* pp. 239-240.
10. Cf. Giovanni A. Bianca, *Il Cinema e l'Astrazione nell'Arte* (Padova, 1964), pp. 151-157.
11. Cf. Arnold Hauser, *"The Social History of Art* (New York, 1958), Vol. 4, pp. 246, 253-254, 257.
12. Alan R. Solomon, in *Catalogue for the U.S.A. in Biennale XXXII,* Copyright by the Jewish Museum (New York, 1964).
13. *Ibid.*
14. Cf. Dewey, *Art As Experience,* pp. 188, 104.
15. *Ibid.,* p. 173.
16. *Ibid.,* p. 337.
17. Jean Dubuffet, "A Commentary," in *Catalogue for the Ivan Albright Retrospective Exhibition* (The Art Institute of Chicago and The Whitney Museum of American Art, 1964-1965), pp. 7-8.
18. Dewey, *Art As Experience,* p. 143.
19. Cf. Gillo Dorfles, "Tecnica e Intenzionalità alla XXXII Biennale," *aut aut,* No. 83 (Settembre 1964), pp. 57-61.
20. Gyorgy Kepes, *The New Landscape in Art and Science* (Chicago, 1956, 1963).
21. Dewey, *Art As Experience,* p. 139.
22. Victorino Tejera, *Art and Human Intelligence,* p. 214.
23. Cf. Wolfgang Steinecke, "Kranichstein—Geschichte, Idee, Ergebnisse," *Darmstädter Beiträge zur Neuen Musik,* IV (1962), 21-22.
24. Cf. "The Changing Guard," *The Times Literary Supplement,* September 3, 1964, pp. 775-789; and Jacques Legrand, "Max Bense et le Groupe de Stuttgart," *Critique,* XXI, No. 218 (Juillet, 1965), 619-628.
25. Cf. Steinecke, *op. cit.,* p. 22.
26. Cf. John Cage, *Silence* (Middletown, Conn. 1961), pp. 10-12, 181.
27. Cf. Bernard Rudofsky, *Architecture Without Architects* (New York, 1964).
28. Esther McCoy, "Avant-Garde Architecture," *Arts in Society,* III, No. 2 (1965), 166.
29. John M. Johansen, "The Avant-Garde in Architecture Today," *ibid.,* pp. 171, 172.
30. John Cage, quoted by Walter Terry, "The Avant-Garde in Dance," *ibid.,* p. 183.
31. Cf. Thom Gunn, "William Carlos Williams," *Encounter,* XXV, No. 1 (July 1965), 67-74.
32. Henry Rago, "Foreword," *Poetry* (October-November, 1962), p. iii.
33. Dewey, *Art As Experience,* p. 133.
34. Cf. Michel Butor in interview in *aut aut,* No. 68, pp. 170-171.
35. Cf. my "Butor and the Book," *Journal of Aesthetics and Art Criticism,* XXIII, No. 1 (Fall, 1964), 159-165.
36. Cf. Pierre Boulez, "Sonate, Que me Veux-Tu?" *Perspectives of New Music,* I, No. 2 (Spring, 1963), 33-34.
37. Cf. Boulez, "Musikdenken Heute 1," *Darmstädter Beiträge zur Neuen Musik,* V (1963), 16.
38. Cf. Kenneth Rexroth, *One Hundred Poems from the Japanese* (New York, 1964), p. x.

39. Cf. Wylie Sypher, *Loss of the Self in Modern Literature and Art,* (New York, 1964), pp. 64-70.
40. *Ibid.,* pp. 5, 68-70, 110, 128-129, 133.
41. John Cage, *Silence,* pp. 161, 8, 46.
42. D. W. Gotshalk, *Art and the Social Order* (Chicago, 1947), pp. 17, 207. Also Dover paperback, 1962.
43. T. W. Adorno, *Philosophie der Neuen Musik* (Tübingen, 1949), p. 87.
44. Horace M. Kallen, *Art and Freedom* (New York, 1942), p. xiv.
45. John M. Johansen, "The Avant-Garde in Architecture Today," *Arts in Society,* III, No. 2 (1965), 170-171.
46. Dewey, *Art As Experience,* pp. 343, 348.
47. D. T. Suzuki, *Zen and Japanese Culture* (New York, 1959).
48. H. S. Hisamatsu, *Zen and Fine Arts* (Kyoto, 1958).

SOCIAL SCIENCE AND SOCIAL NORMS

by Clifford Barrett

It would seem of as great importance to scrutinize the reliability of norms one is applying, as that of one or another way of applying them. Actually, however, a contrary procedure is more usual—for many will comply and insist upon the compliance of others, with particular norms of inference, valuation and action, stake principal hopes upon their soundness, and perhaps devote years of effort to their meticulous application, all with scarcely a serious effort to determine just how probable it may be that the favored norms really warrant any such trust. There are some areas of interest within which this way of proceeding may arise from the implicit faith of believers in a divinely revealed sanction of certain norms. But elsewhere and more widely, doubtless it is accepted in preference to confronting difficulties of critical inquiry on as fundamental a level as the justifying grounds of one's group's governing ideas and valuations, established aims, policies, and institutional systems.

That many should feel such hesitancy is not strange—much as it is understandable that less experienced climbers are likely to feel uncomfortable with the thought that they should continually watch their foothold. But it is surprising to find experts who appear oblivious to any such need. We must suppose the experienced investigator—for instance in a field of social interest such as economics, politics, or law—has other reasons than intellectual timidity for his reluctance to press his inquiries into basic normative issues, toward their eventual untanglement. It might be expected that he would consider critically the norms he employs, from the standpoint of their adequacy to deal with more essential aspects of his subject matter—especially the distinctive aspects which uniquely differentiate the nature of its phenomena. In social inquiry, for example, will not the competent investigator critically scrutinize his norms from the standpoint of their adequacy to treat the ground-assumptions of fact and valuation, whatever they may be, upon which a given society bases its whole structure of working norms?

A familiar reply to suggestions that he do so, has taken the form of an appeal to *fact*. Is it not the business of the scientist in social as well as other areas, to describe accurately what *is*—not to imagine or attempt to judge what *ought to be?* How can anyone measure or verify a society's prevailing conceptions of what ought to be, or establish the real *rightness* of its principal norms when these are shaped in terms of some imaginatively projected ideal aims? Since it is the function of social norms to properly direct thinking and acting toward desirable future consequences, they must be based upon speculative estimates of the potentials of people and things. At a particular time, tests for the soundness of a norm virtually must amount to tests of reliability for whatever predictions of future consequences assuredly are to be anticipated from its use. In the case of social norms which involve valuations, expressive of varyingly *desirable* aspects to be experienced in the consequences, matters are further complicated by a need to weigh predictions in terms of what will prove generally pleasing or otherwise in the tumultuous world of human feelings and desires. In short, social norms implying valuations must be recognized as constructions shaped by human imagination to implement its ideal ends—norms seemingly well-adapted to perform their function of insuring satisfactions of needs in a near or more distant future—hence in a still only imaginatively constructed world. Is it strange that such normative creations should vary radically with times and localities? But is it not also clear that issues of real validity or of verification in the case of these diverse normative idealizations that imagination projects as standard criteria for social behavior, must lie quite without the ambit of true *scientific* inquiry? It is of course unfortunate if this frequently leaves the treatment of powerful social sentiments chiefly to the sentimentalists, who may know little of what sound scientific thinking means—but we are asked, is it not the only course open to the responsible social scientist?

Affirmative answers on the part of a good many social scientists have been supported in at least two ways—one, by the familiar assertion that it is the function of true science to describe accurately and classify *facts* as they are found. It is not to interpret their significance or attempt their valuation in terms of human interests. Hence, critical problems of norms which involve questions of justifiable valuations, are not germane to social study which deserves to be called "scientific." Let inquiries that would be worthy of being valued and trusted by men as truly "scientific," sternly eschew all consideration of basic validity in social valuations, devoting themselves instead wholeheartedly to facts—especially those susceptible of exact objective observation and statistical tabulation.

A second support for a radically factualist attitude has been found in a differing argument which sees no serious difficulty at all about the way to determine a society's proper valuational norms. It may indeed be the case that inquiry entirely faithful to scientific method in such fields as law, economics, and politics, cannot remain altogether oblivious to the validity of common norms of human significance and valuation. But these norms need only be tested by the plainly observable facts of relevant situations. Indeed, sound valuational norms are precisely those which have been *derived from correctly established facts*—and not from any ideology or anyone's imaginative idealizations.

Both of these ways of escape for the social scientist from questions of critical justification—whether for social norms or those he himself employs in treating social phenomena—are confronted by certain difficulties. One of these, and perhaps the most damaging, arises from the essential nature of the "facts" to which such arguments would ascribe finality. "Fact" is, of course, an ambiguous word, likely to be used one moment as a designation for what is *really the case*—but the next as a name for what the speaker, or his group or age, on some ground deemed convincing, *thinks is really the case*. Taken as a synonym for "final reality," "facts" would be indubitably certain—*if* we could also certainly possess any of them. On the other hand, taken as *interpretative constructions* from material of empirical impressions and assumptions of coherent thought, and tested for reliability by criteria that seem convincing in terms of the prevailing idea-system of a time and place, our "known facts" may be numerous, of indispensable worth, and often, in all probability, most reliable constructions —but never surely beyond possible need of future reconsideration and revision. Now either of these usages of the word might be well enough if adhered to consistently—the trouble comes when they are confused, making "fact" mean *actual reality* at one moment, and at the next what seems *a reliable way of construing* what is real. Surely no age has seen greater alterations in the "plain" or "indubitable" facts of the past, than our own.

It is an elementary recognition that our experienced and known facts—which are the only ones we may well consider—in any literal sense, never are simply "given," or "found" ready-made for the taking. All are, of course, conditioned by human modes of perception, shaped and defined in terms of prevailing systems of ideas, as well as verified by whatever criteria of truth and value such a system assumes and approves. Assuredly this does not mean that all constructions of fact are altogether factitious, or that all are to be dismissed in a spirit of dogmatic scepticism as equally unreliable. What it does indicate is that trust in any facts must be at root trust in the justifiability of the *systematic grounds* that have determined its specific formulation and acceptance. And these systematic grounds can only be such through normative requirements which demand that one construction rather than some other shall be accepted as actual "fact." Thus trust in facts, far from constituting a substitute for critical scrutiny of norms or appraisal of their reliability, necessarily turns out to be trust in the particular systematic norms apart from which no idea of *these* particular facts would exist in men's minds. Indeed, without some systematic norms for their formulation and acceptance, there would clearly be no notion of facts among human beings, only manifold unorganized impressions—but then we would scarcely be human beings.

My point is, that *fact* and *norm* are both essentially systematic terms—both are inseparably dependent within a people's total idea-system—both confront the social scientist who seeks any fundamental understanding of his subject matter with what are at root identical problems of verification. These pertain first, to whether a particular fact or norm adequately satisfies what a system of ideas—scientific, religious, economic, political, legal, *etc.*—requires. But further, they pertain to whether requirements of the system rest upon normative assumptions that are actually justifiable.

Within the whole prevailing idea-system of a time and place, all recognized facts are construed in terms of particular segmental systems of interest—all are facts within more or less specialized frames of reference, facts of one kind or another. So it happens that the "factual world" to which a science of economics, politics, or law is germane, is quite a different one than the "factual world" to which a science of chemistry, physics, or astronomy pertains. There may of course be much in common, but all construe their facts in systematic terms—which means with reference to different, though obviously related, systems. The facts, as they are construed in terms of a particular system, bear characteristics of the system—and this, not merely as superficial aspects, but as essential characteristics without which they simply would not be the kind of facts they are. Thus, for example, beyond characteristics of a physical system, such as space-time relations, or motion and causality, *biological* facts possess essential characteristics of a recognized system of specifically *organic* relationships. They are not less real facts for this, however, and the biologist who sought to avoid consideration of aspects of his facts which were distinctively organic characteristics would not be serving science, but effacing his field of inquiry. And surely it cannot be the demand of a truly scientific attitude that one ignore what is peculiar to the subject matter of his field, but, rather, that he seek adequate ways of dealing effectively with what may be unique to it.

One distinctive characteristic of much of the factual subject matter with which an investigator must deal in any area of *social* inquiry is the presence of human motivation as a shaping cause of relationships, attitudes and activities. Irrespective of any hypothesis one may choose to hold regarding a "freedom of will" at the basis of motivation, it is clear that in no presently recognizable way can this motivation of men in society be systematized in any such regular order, for example, as that evident in chemical reactions. Thus, while the chemist may find norms for his judgments and choices (*e.g.*, of hypotheses) that are implied in a rigidly regular system of relations—imaginatively idealized as universal by his forerunners and subsequently abundantly tested—successful norms for a social science cannot well be grounded in assumptions of any such predictably undeviating, or mechanical, regularity. They must be established upon predictable agreements of a different kind, i.e., predictable motivating values.

Understood in terms of the relations of a system which involves motivation, recognized facts acquire a new dimension as an intrinsic part of their nature. That is, they acquire future projections—the recognized facts becoming *what* they are, to a large extent, by virtue of more or less desirable potentials of future consequence. Bradley pointed out that we recognize a thing as a factual reality, rather than illusion, through its continuing to be what it was—and nothing is more familiar than Bergson's brilliant work in showing the large place memory holds in establishing all factual knowledge. But some manner of imaginative construction of its near, if not distant, future being and significance is similarly indispensable to every construction in thought and experience which we designate as "a fact."

This future dimension in our known facts doubtless is due to their being constituted both by the nature of what is known and our particular human way of knowing and taking interest in it. It is characteristic of all living beings that their actions are somehow directed toward the future, though with simpler creatures presumably with no conscious purpose on their part. Higher animals frequently show measures of foresight. Human beings, however, possess a further degree of mentality—of which the crucial test, in William James's phrase, is a capacity to select future ends and choose means for their attainment. For man, as Cassirer said, "to think of the future and to live in the future, is a necessary part of his nature." Implied in this are human capacities for deliberate valuations. Man's life of thought and action—rather than of "torpid stupor"—is due to his shaping, not merely some *single* image for the future, toward which he might then remain passive, but numerous and diverse images. Among these he may attempt value-judgments of more and less desirable. Thereafter he may direct his actions accordingly—earning the distinction of being an intelligent self-directing creature. Further, among the possible images is that which would be *best* for the future—one in terms of which other images are to be appraised relatively. True, there may be scant hope of achieving this *best* state of affairs in its entirety at any foreseeable date. But it serves to provide a criterion by which to determine the relative merits of more easily accessible ends and courses of action. In short, it permits translation of preferred ideal-ends into working objectives, with meanings that pass beyond temporary requirements of prudence to more comprehensive considerations of policy—and perhaps occasionally to imperatives of wisdom.

Norms are by nature guides—their claims of validity imply preferable future consequences for judgments, valuations and actions which comply with them. Difficulties in their verification by a scientific method have been described in diverse ways which usually in the end come back to this—how can constructions of imagination, which are not observable facts at all in an objective sense, ever be scientifically verified? What I have wished to suggest here is that the social scientist is faced by remarkably similar and to a considerable extent the same difficulties, whether he attempts to verify in any basic way, either the norms—political, legal, economic—that live in a people's dominant idea-system, or the constructions of fact which live in the system. Indeed, the factual constructions depend upon the normative assumptions in a system of thinking in terms of which they are effected. This does not mean that neither norms nor facts can be verified with a high degree of probability. But it does suggest that the impassable gulf frequently supposed to separate the soundly verifiable facts of a scientific social inquiry, from the gossamer-winged ideal norms fashioned by a society's imagination, is itself one of the more unfortunate products of imagination. But why should imagination, in its saner manifestations, be equated with mere fancy or wishful thinking? Has it not been responsible for every major advance since the Stone Age—each in turn proceeding through imaginative insight—in the case of social attitudes and institutional life, insight which revised or displaced old valuational norms for new. For whatever we may think of it, we may hardly deny that our civilization, as Professor Tsanoff has observed, "is what it is and where it is because of our choice and scale of values."

There is slight room for question that it must always be so. The pertinent question is why society should be deprived by the social scientist of a penetrating examination of the norms it lives by, from those who possess competent skill and experience in critical investigation. It was an error of the seventeenth century, that it tended to equate the meaning of "scientific spirit" with the use of a specific and limited methodology—useful in some areas, but absurd in the borrowed applications of "social physics." Is it not the essence of scientific wisdom that everywhere method follows the requirements for sound and adequate understanding? It is not the function of a method of inquiry to determine what is to be examined or neglected in the basic nature of its subject matter, but to provide a competent means of examination for whatever of consequence is present to be explored. Scientific method has seen many revisions and enlargements to achieve effective competence in distinctive fields. Why should the social scientist remain timid or unimaginative in developing fundamental adaptations which will enable him to deal cogently and critically with normative issues of his phenomena—even to the basic value-assumptions from which they come?

PHILOSOPHY AND THE TWO CULTURES

by A. Cornelius Benjamin

No one who has scanned nonfictional books and periodicals in the last four or five years can, I think, fail to be impressed with the increasingly frequent appearance of the phrase "the two cultures." The expression is not restricted to literary journals, where it would seem quite appropriate, but is found in scientific articles, book publishers' lists, college catalogues, and is mentioned with great frequency in commencement addresses. It is always in quotes, of course, since it is well known to have been created by Sir Charles P. Snow in his Rede Lecture, *The Two Cultures and the Scientific Revolution,*[1] given at Cambridge University in 1959. One naturally assumes that those who quote the phrase know what Snow had in mind when he employed it, though the context in which they use it often indicates confusion, and sometimes complete ignorance, as to what he presumably meant. That this misunderstanding is not completely without justification I shall attempt to show in the following paper, since I am convinced that while Snow was wrestling with a genuine problem, he was not at all clear in his own mind either as to what the problem was or how it was to be solved.

According to precedent, the lecture was published in England as a paper-covered pamphlet the day after it was given. There were few reviews, some editorial comments, and short excerpts which were published in *Encounter*. Snow received some interesting private letters, but on the whole the lecture attracted little immediate attention. However, according to Snow's own report,[2] by the time a year had passed, articles, references, letters, and comments began to appear in great numbers from all parts of the world. Some of these were commendatory, some personally abusive, some of them stupid, and one essay was so critical that it almost resulted in a law suit.[3] When the volume of comment finally became formidable, Snow decided to take action and attempt to clarify his original point of view. His severest critics had objected to the word "culture"; many were unhappy with the number "two"; no one, he says, complained about the definite article. (I propose to criticize all three.) He resolved, therefore, to republish in a single volume the original lecture as given, his reactions to some of the criticisms of this material, and a general restatement of his position, admitting certain errors, omissions, and misleading emphases in his first formulation; but defending substantially the point of view he had taken at the outset. The result was the publication of the book mentioned in the footnote above, *The Two Cultures: and A Second Look.*[4]

I

I shall begin by summarizing, I hope not too unfairly, what I understand to be his problem. There have been so many misleading statements of his position that I hesitate to venture still another. But he at least took his start from the distinction, well recognized by educators and the general public alike, between a technical and a liberal education, and tried to account for, and perhaps eliminate, the hostility so often exhibited between the two groups of people who have had the respective modes of training. Sir Eric Ashby calls it the conflict between two powerful social forces—"the influence of the utilitarians and the cult of the practical man on the one hand, and the influence of the classical humanist and the cult of the scholar-gentleman on the other."[5] While this is partly correct I think it is not an accurate statement of Snow's position. The honorific aspect of the words "scholar-gentleman" would probably receive his unqualified approval, but the derogatory suggestion of the words "practical" and "utilitarian" would seem inappropriate when applied to many scientists as Snow would characterize them and even as most people would describe them today. Snow's problem was that in advanced Western society educated people (I shall use this somewhat vague term for the present) are becoming sharply divided into two groups who have so little in common intellectually that they can scarcely converse with each other. This division among men of knowledge is not only increasingly disturbing to our normal social life—such as carrying on an intelligent conversation at a dinner party where representatives of both groups are present—but, what is much more important, it makes planning for the future of our civilization impossible. For the solutions of the social, political, and moral issues before us are now seen to be increasingly dependent not on the one group *or* the other, but on some sort of cooperative action between the two. A method must be found, therefore, for dispelling the antagonism between the groups, informing the ignorant in each group of what is well known in the other, and establishing a method for bridging the gap between them. Only in this way can enlightened choices be made concerning the kind of society in which we hope our children may live.

The response to Snow's original lecture, slow though it was in appearing, convinced the author of two things. In the first place, "if a nerve had been touched almost simultaneously in different intellectual societies, in different parts of the world, the ideas which produced the response couldn't possibly be original. Original ideas do not carry at that speed. . . . The ideas were in the air. Anyone, anywhere, had only to choose a form of words. Then—click, the trigger was pressed."[6] In the second place, Snow was convinced that there must be something in the ideas. This does not mean that they are necessarily right or could not have been expressed in different forms, but that "contained in them or hidden beneath them, there is something which people all over the world suspect to be relevant to present actions."[7]

This, then, was Snow's problem. First, to acquaint the general public with the existence of these sharply differentiated groups of educated people lacking a common vocabulary and a common subject matter, who have long recognized their status but have done nothing about it. Snow hoped to gain this end by finding appropriate words to characterize each of the groups, and thus to clarify the difference which separates them. Second, to show that the future of society can be shaped only by cooperative efforts on the part of these semi-hostile groups. This conflict, he argues, is not new but is part of the *Zeitgeist*, and its transparency is recognized as soon as people are made aware of it.

II

There seems to be no doubt whatsoever, at least in Snow's mind, as to who the people are who constitute one division of this educated group. They are the natural scientists, particularly the physical scientists. Snow is himself a physicist, has pursued research at Cambridge University for many years, and was scientific adviser for the British Government during the war. As to the other group, Snow never makes himself clear; he calls them the "literary intellectuals." Since Snow is not only a physicist but a novelist of some repute, having written, according to the last report, nine novels, which have sold moderately well, there is some reason to suppose that he is really using himself as a pattern for bifurcating the educated public into a scientific part which corresponds to his technical interests, and a literary part which represents his creative writing capacities and his frequent references to the current world of fiction.

In spite of Snow's elaborate explanation of why he chose the phrase, "the two cultures," to describe these two groups, I think his decision was most unfortunate. Offhand I cannot think of a single word in the area of his general problem which is so wrought with ambiguity and vagueness as the word "culture."[8] Even small dictionaries give six or seven definitions of the term. If we exclude some of the technical uses, such as tillage of the soil, the cultivation of a particular crop, e.g., oyster culture, and the biological growth of bacteria in a nutrient medium, we are left with two definitions, both of which Snow considers to be involved in his notion.

According to the first of these, culture is "intellectual development, development of the mind."[9] Snow admits that this definition has often carried overtones of a deep and ambiguous sort, and there is an aspect of "refinement," not clearly expressed in the definition, which leads us when we ask who is cultured to find that the needle points by an extraordinary coincidence to ourselves. This aspect of the definition I wish to disregard for the moment, since I hope to return to it later. But to define culture as intellectual development cannot possibly serve any useful purpose in distinguishing his two forms of culture, since we have already characterized both groups as educated people, and what we need is some way of distinguishing not the *manner* of their education but the *content*.

Snow's second definition of culture is the commonly accepted anthropological one: "a group of persons living in the same environment, linked by common habits, common assumptions, a common way of life."[10] This description seems to me to be even less illuminating as a basis for distinguishing his two groups of intellectuals. To establish the fact that physical scientists exhibit a common culture in this sense would be extremely difficult, and, fortunately for the reader, I shall not make the attempt.[11] Of course they use generally the same methods and make the same presuppositions in carrying on their studies —this goes without saying, and is true for the literary intellectuals as well. But I see no evidence that either scientists or literary intellectuals have a distinctive cultural environment or a distinctive philosophy of life. In fact the cold war has done something to science which would have seemed impossible thirty years ago—it has developed a geography of science. Prior to this time science had been an outstanding example of an international, interracial, intersectarian enterprise—a cooperative institution on a worldwide basis. To the extent to which the cultures making up this institution became fragmented, differently constituted, and at odds with one another cooperation ceased; cultural similarities in scientific interests were not strong enough to prevent the divisive influences of ideological disagreements. So, too, in the case of the literary intellectuals. Scientists do not have a distinctive culture, nor do literary intellectuals. I do not see, therefore, how Snow can use the anthropological meaning of the term "culture" to differentiate his two groups on the basis of their respective patterns of living.

What Snow wanted, I believe, and what is contained in still another definition of "culture" is that aspect of "refinement" to which reference was made above. Snow does not give such a definition in either of his essays, though he could have found one in Webster. But he does make a subtle reference to it in a brief article, "The Two Cultures," published three years before the Rede lecture.[12] Here he quotes the mathematician G. H. Hardy: " 'It is odd,' says Hardy, 'that when we hear about the intellectuals nowadays it doesn't include people like me and J. J. Thomsom and Rutherford.' "[13] And Snow would probably add, "Nor does it include me in my capacity as a physicist." Snow and the other scientists were irked by the fact that according to the prevailing conception only literary men are intellectual. The Oxford dictionary defines a liberal education as an education fit for a gentleman. Yet this irritation at being excluded from the intelligentsia manifested itself in a strange way. For in this same article in *The New Statesman and Nation* Snow points out that the scientific culture views with indifference all philosophy, but especially metaphysics. The philosopher whom he has in mind is Samuel Alexander, and this time it is Rutherford speaking: "When you think about all of the years you have been talking about these things, Alexander, what does it amount to? *Hot air,* nothing but *hot air!*"[14] This, says Snow, is the opinion of contemporary scientists. They regard it as a major intellectual virtue to know what not to think about. But the embarrassment arises from the fact that Alexander, by no stretch of the imagination, could be called a scientist; nor was he a literary intellectual as Snow defines the term. Yet, as I indicated above, Snow is extremely vague in his definition of this latter group, and if there are to be only two cultures Alexander would certainly be more closely allied to the literary group than to the scientists. But why should the scientists want to be identified with the intellectuals if their products are frequently nothing but hot air? Presumably the scientists have only two choices: either to be intellectuals and find that they often have very undesirable bedfellows, or to be nonintellectuals and discover that they are then classified not as gentlemen, but as gadgeteers and pebble-pickers.

Thus Snow appeared to be unable to find a definition of culture which would place the scientists among the social elite, and hence would guarantee that element of "refinement" and prestige to which he made previous reference. The fact that Webster defines the term in one place as "the enlightenment and refinement of taste acquired by intellectual and aesthetic training"[15] does not seem to satisfy Snow in spite of his presumed knowledge of the musical competence of a Teller or an Einstein, and his awareness of the deep appreciation of music exhibited by many scientists. These appeared to him to be isolated cases, and he wonders how much of the traditional (literary) culture gets through to scientists in general,[16] and to what degree the interests of scientists often extend into the area of religious, moral, political, legal, and humanitarian values. He is forced to the conclusion that although scientists might have high competence in matters of social policy, they are not generally recognized as authorities in this area and are rarely consulted when questions of value come up for decision.

That Snow finally solved his problem by a bit of skillful linguistic legerdemain would, perhaps, be too severe a criticism. But that he *apparently* solved it to the satisfaction of most people by the introduction of the weasel word "culture" hardly seems deniable. In Jacques Barzun's review [17] of Aldous Huxley's last book he states that the phrase "the two cultures" has become a "too successful cliché"; it apparently solves many problems but really solves none. In fact if some of its presuppositions are accepted it actually prevents the essential difficulty from being met. I shall argue, therefore, that Snow, by defining science in an unnecessarily restrictive way, and by defining the literary intellectuals so amorphously as to leave the reader completely in the dark as to whom they include has confused the issue rather than clarified it. Let me list, first, the errors which Snow himself discovered in his first formulation of the problem, when he reexamined it in his "second look."

III

Among the most important of the mistakes which Snow hastens to correct in the second essay is his original restriction of the number of cultures to *two*. His thinking on this problem can best be explained in his own words taken from the first lecture:

> The number 2 is a very dangerous number: that is why the dialectic is a dangerous process. Attempts to divide anything into two ought to be regarded with much suspicion. I have thought a long time about going in for further refinements: but in the end I have decided against. I was searching for something a little more than a dashing metaphor, a good deal less than a cultural map: and for these purposes the two cultures is about right, and subtilizing any more would bring more disadvantages than it is worth.[18]

It is here, I believe, that Snow committed his greatest error: the important but highly complicated problem which he was considering cannot be solved by a "dashing metaphor." Metaphors solve nothing: they frequently illuminate; they often confuse; and by the looseness of their terminology they suggest quite different interpretations of the issue being considered. On the other hand, "cultural maps" *do* involve subtilizing. As we have already seen, the word "culture" demands precise definition before it can function as a clarifying term in the problem, and as we shall see in a minute the word "two" proves to have been a positive error. The result is that in order to solve his problem Snow will have to subtilize about the term "literary intellectual"; about the difference between pure and applied sciences; about the problem of human values—and he will find himself, in spite of his wishes, deep in the intricacies of philosophy. It seems obvious to me that the world-wide controversy which was generated by his first lecture was due to the fact that he chose to solve his problem by a dashing metaphor which lent itself to so many varied interpretations that his critics insisted on a more analytic approach, in spite of the subtleties which this would necessarily involve. His commentators were not surprised at his disclosure of a complex problem of social control which was urgently in need of solution; they knew that this problem existed and that it was the result of the rapid growth of science, particularly in its increasingly practical role. But they also recognized the magnitude of the problem, and were genuinely disturbed that a glib phrase could be proposed to slay, at one blow, such a huge monster.

In Snow's second account he explains why he divided his educated group into *two* cultures:

> I think . . . that writing as an Englishman made me insensitive to something which may, within a few years, propel the argument in another direction or which conceivably may already have started to do just that. I have been increasingly impressed by a body of intellectual opinion, forming itself, without any kind of lead or conscious direction, under the surface of this debate. . . . This body of opinion seems to come from intellectual persons in a variety of fields—social-history, sociology, demography, political science, economics, governments (in the American academic sense), psychology, medicine, and social arts such as architecture. It seems a mixed bag: but there is an inner consistency. All of them are concerned with how human beings are living or have lived—and concerned, not in terms of legend, but in terms of fact. I am not implying that they agree with each other, but in their approach to cardinal problems—such as the human effects of the scientific revolution, which is the fighting point of this whole affair—they display, at least, a family resemblance.
>
> I ought, I see now, to have expected this. I haven't much excuse for not doing so. I have been in close intellectual contact with social historians most of my life: they have influenced me a good deal: their recent researches were the basis for a good many of my statements. But nevertheless I was slow to observe the development of what, in terms of our formula, is becoming something like a third culture.[19]

While this has not commonly been called a "culture" in this country, it has long been recognized as a legitimate study in spite of some of the dubious subjects, such as medicine and architecture, which are included by Snow but do not quite fit into our pattern. I happen to prefer the term "behavioral" to "social" to characterize these studies, but this is a matter of no great import. Now I do not propose to involve myself at this point in the issue of scientism, i.e., whether the methods of the natural sciences are applicable to the behavioral sciences with sufficient success to warrant the latter being included in the sciences in the basic sense. But Snow's pronouncement clearly indicates that in his initial attempt to bifurcate the world he felt either that the natural sciences were the only sciences, or that human, preferential behavior did not constitute an element of experience which had enough importance to be classified among the basic cultures. This omission I think was a serious one, but he deserves credit in his "second look" for recognizing that the behavioral studies might be at least an embryonic third type of culture, whether scientific or nonscientific.

He explains both his overemphasis on the sharpness of the division into two cultures and his failure to recognize a possible third culture by saying that he was speaking as an Englishman, educated in England, and that he was strongly influenced by continental education, particularly German. In both systems the student, usually early in his career, makes a choice between a technical education and a literary one, which never overlap, and which leave him consequently blind to half of what constitutes the intellectual competence of the truly educated man.[20] However, in America Snow discovers, apparently to his amazement, not only that many students are exposed to both cultures but that in technological schools, whose curricula would presumably be largely centered on sciences in general, and on practical sciences in particular, extensive opportunities are given to all students to pursue education in humanities, literature, and philosophy. Indeed, in at least one technological school[21] a full doctorate program is now offered, which is designed precisely to bridge the two cultures. Thus, in the United States the break between the two forms is not so sharp as he had led his readers to suppose. Students are not only given opportunities but actually urged to adopt curricula whose precise goal is to eliminate the situation which Snow is deploring.

Snow's third modification in his original point of view is not in the reference to a further distinction but in the apparent abandonment of one which had seemed essential when he first defined the two cultures —that between pure and applied science. He introduced this by suggesting that there is a very important difference between an industrial revolution and a scientific revolution. Part of the social crisis today lies in the fact that the old mechanical science, which determined the industrial revolution of the eighteenth century, is so different from today's electronics, atomic energy, and automation, that we have no way of predicting what kind of technological revolution the newer science will produce. But in Snow's second thoughts he seems to suggest abandoning entirely the distinction between pure science and technology, at least as a difference between two kinds of science. His grounds for this rejection lie in the practical difficulty in deciding whether any particular example of scientific investigation is pure or applied. In this possibility of confusing a given case I should certainly agree with him.

But that the fundamental distinction between them exists, and even remains in his own mind, is clear from the following quotation: "The scientific process has two motives: one is to understand the natural world, the other is to control it. Either of these motives may be dominant in any individual scientist; fields of science may draw their original impulses from one or the other."[22] Pure science, in other words, is the pursuit of truth concerning the structure and operation of the world with no regard whatsoever for the use to which this knowledge is to be put in the way of making men happier or the world better; it is the satisfaction of an intellectual curiosity and is much like solving crossword puzzles except that its problems are posed by nature and not by man. Applied science is the modification of the world toward the attainment of our goals and ideals.

But while this both defines and justifies the distinction between pure and applied science it does not remove the ambiguity in the term "applied science." What we should *like* to say is that there remains the distinction between the "pure" applied scientist and the "applied" applied scientist. Does the applied scientist actually change the world as a result of his knowledge of pure science, or does he merely show us how this can be done in case it is so desired? Unfortunately the term "applied scientist" has come to be used to describe both the scientist who indulges in applied research, but who makes no changes whatsoever in the world, and the artisan, the practitioner, and even the professional man, who actually manipulate nature by introducing the instruments which will create the desired ends. Unless this distinction is maintained we shall continually confuse engineering schools with manufacturing companies, schools of business and public administration with business enterprises, and medical schools with medical clinics. The distinction is very important because the solution to the problem of the social responsibilities of the scientist rests upon it. But into this question I cannot go at this point.

Snow is certainly to be criticized for not making abundantly clear whether he does or does not accept this basic distinction. But what is of more concern is his failure to recognize that the terms "applied science" and its equivalent, "technology," are both subject to a serious ambiguity. If I might be allowed, for the moment, to speak in an oversimplified language, I should say that pure science attempts to discover causal relations between events in the world. Now a pure science becomes an applied science by a very simple transformation: if the effect is something which does not exist at a certain time and place but we should *like* to have it exist, then we employ the cause as an instrument (provided it is under our control) by which we create the desired effect. Thus cause-and-effect relations in pure science become means-end relations in applied science, and what determines the transformation is the fact that something which does not exist is desired by man. The notion of applied science is meaningless apart from the notion of value.

In summary, I have shown that Snow tried to raise the prestige of scientists by calling them "cultured." In order to do this he had to define by a dashing metaphor a new culture—a scientific culture—which proved to be confusing since it became contrasted with an English and continental culture much more narrowly conceived than the broad, humanistic culture of our American colleges and universities. Then, almost by accident, he discovered a culture which he had previously overlooked—the behavioral sciences. Finally, although his main problem was to determine the social role of the scientist, he equivocated on the distinction between the pure and applied sciences.

I am of the opinion that the real source of Snow's confusion is his failure to recognize that the problem which he has undertaken to solve is a philosophical one. So far as I can detect after several readings of Snow's serious writings he mentions the word "philosophy" in the derogatory context above, where he refers to Rutherford's comment on Alexander's writing, but rarely elsewhere, and then in settings which are merely incidental. However, according to almost any of the traditional conceptions of philosophy what Snow is doing *is* philosophy. He is examining the universe and trying to discover "parts," which he wants to call "cultures," and which he wishes to interrelate into a whole. Many would agree that this is what Snow is doing, and that the results are, indeed, "hot air." If this is true the most expedient solution would be not to wait for Snow to take a "third look" at the problem, but to advise him to abandon the two cultures completely and start again from the beginning, this time philosophically. I am afraid such a suggestion is too late. Barzun was obviously right in saying that the phrase "the two cultures" has become a too successful cliché; people are going to continue to use it in spite of anything we can now do. This is discouraging, for the problem which Snow has raised is not only complicated but urgently in need of a solution. As he says, the widespread reaction to his thesis clearly indicates that the ideas contained in it are considered by people all over the world to be relevant to the present social situation. It is a pity, therefore, that we must first undo all that Snow has done before we can face the problem in an unprejudiced manner.

What general conclusions can we draw? Snow has grossly oversimplified the problem, and some further explorations and careful analyses will be required in order to resolve some of the resulting difficulties.

Snow is prone to metaphorical thinking: the literary intellectuals represent a culture; so also, by a broadening meaning of the word, do the scientists. The behavioral scientists, newly discovered by Snow, exhibit many common interests and methods; let us also give them the status of a culture. And even on the negative side the vagueness of the cultural metaphor prevents him from making up his mind as to whether the pure sciences are culturally different from the applied. And, finally, philosophy is denied cultural status simply because Snow does not realize that when cultures are defined, there is the further cultural task of integrating them into a unified whole.

But because of these confusions in Snow's thought, there are many misleading interpretations of his position. For example, many of those who adopt the "two culture" phraseology clearly suppose him to have set up a fact-value dichotomy: to scientists is assigned the study of facts; to humanists the study of values. I do not think that this was Snow's intention, in spite of the fact that it offers him certain advantages in his use of the cultural metaphor. It tends to destroy the social superiority of the humanists over the scientists, so much resented by the latter group. For valued objects are clearly objects—be they the abstractions of logic and mathematics, mass-energy, life, or human behavior—and these lie in the field of the sciences if the area is given proper breadth. Another advantage is the fact that the scientist can see his subject matter as not completely value-free, but as a value potential. Every fact is a value possibility—even if only to be known, to be painted, to be the subject of a poem, or to be the object of religious worship. Thus the scientist is in a position to provide the humanist with material for embellishing life and emphasizing its characteristically valuational aspects. Snow seems to be rightly disturbed by our failure to create individuals who can be, so to speak, doubly cultured in the sense that they always see the interrelationships of facts and values. But if his initial examination of the world had been less hasty, less tied up with unfortunate terminology, less prejudiced by nationalistic points of view, and more empirical in its approach, he would have discovered that facts and values are integral parts of our total culture, interrelated in a very complicated map, and that he has separated them only through a vicious abstraction which will plague him to the end of his days.

IV

Anyone who is to solve the problem which Snow has set up must first realize that his task is, indeed, a philosophical one, and must be undertaken with full knowledge of the scope and complexities of the enterprise. As we have abundantly seen, a dashing metaphor will not work: a detailed map of the universe is required. Metaphors are crude and suggestive rather than straightforward; maps have not only precise boundaries but they locate areas in their relations one to another.

One finds it difficult to understand why Snow, who realizes that the problem can be solved only by better education, refuses to recognize that our schools, particularly our universities, have from their inception provided us with highly accurate maps of the universe, reflecting not only man's aims and ideals but his accomplishments and findings as well. He says, in fact, that we can do something about the problem. "The chief means open to us is education—education mainly in the primary and secondary schools, but also in colleges and universities. There is no excuse for letting another generation be as vastly ignorant, or as devoid of understanding and sympathy, as we ourselves."[23] Why, then, should we not turn to our universities for light? The great diversity exhibited in the curricula of our institutions of higher learning should cause us neither to lose faith in their reliability as indicators of what there is in the universe that is worth examining, nor to despair because of the complexity of the problem to be solved. Snow has more or less unconsciously uncovered important areas of study, but he has misnamed them and confused their interrelationships.

In this concluding section I shall venture to list the main fields of inquiry to which we must turn for the solution to the problem of social control and related issues. I shall not use the word "culture" to designate these areas, for reasons which I hope have been made clear in the preceding pages. For the same reason I shall not speak of the cultivation of these areas, but shall use the accepted academic word "disciplines" to designate scholarly investigations into these fields of inquiry. Our task, then, is to produce a pattern of the most general areas of the universe, and a corresponding map of the disciplines by which these areas are to be investigated.

Outstanding among these fields are the sciences as disciplines and their corresponding fields of exploration as subject matter. The recent revolution in mathematics (to which Snow, strangely enough, makes no reference) demands, I think, that we distinguish sharply the natural sciences (biological and physical) from pure mathematics and logic. Similarly I believe that we must, in spite of Snow's reluctance to do so, admit the behavioral sciences into the field of the sciences; certainly they share methods with the natural sciences, yet exhibit their own peculiarities just as mathematical logic both resembles and differs from the natural sciences.

But the sciences are not just sciences—they are pure or applied. Now this distinction is not only in method but subject matter as well. Both the logico-mathematical and the natural sciences are value-free (except insofar as truth itself is a value), but so also are the behavioral sciences, which study values as objective manifestations of preferential behavior. As was suggested above, pure science becomes applied science when effects are seen as ends and causes are interpreted as means. This is true in mathematics, physics, and biology, but it is no less true in the behavioral sciences. Pure behavioral sciences describe existing modes of valuational behavior, and are thus not normative sciences except in the sense that they portray the prevailing norms of a given society. Applied behavioral sciences in their simplest form tell us how to find the instruments by means of which society may be bettered; they thus deal with instrumental values primarily, not with final values. The full-blown applied behavioral sciences are policy-making sciences and attempt to determine the ultimate goals of human living in the many areas of our experience.

However, the field of the applied scientist, whether mathematical logician, naturalist, or sociologist, is not to be confused with that of the special worker—the artisan, the laborer, the technician, the businessman, the agriculturist, the doctor, the lawyer, even the teacher—whose task is to put means to work in order to produce the desired ends, once they have been approved by the social group. Thus we have created a new "culture"—the manipulators—who by skill and knowledge actually transform the world (hopefully) into a better place to live, in which there will be a greater abundance of health, wealth, knowledge, piety, morality, and beauty. Some of these manipulators engage in these activities as trades and professions, by which they earn a living; others pursue them simply as avocations or as instruments for the production of a fuller life—a life which, without them, would be ill, poor, ignorant, sinful, immoral, and surrounded by ugliness.

Among the disciplines which a philosophical map of the universe discloses, perhaps the hardest to distinguish one from the other are the behavioral sciences and the humanities. Snow discovered the former only after a second look; he defined the latter in terms of the "literary intellectuals," and we found that he was quite unclear as to whom this included. He refers most often to men like himself, who are novelists and literary critics. But he obviously means to include a group which is much wider in scope—all those who deal with the basic human values of truth, beauty, morality, piety, law and government, education, health, recreation, and all of the goals which contribute to the well-being of mankind. The problem is that both the behavioral sciences and what are commonly called the "humanities" deal with precisely these same values. How, then, are they to be distinguished?

Since this is a highly controversial issue and many methods for distinguishing the two have been offered in the history of thought, I shall state my view dogmatically.[24] I find it convenient to define the humanities as the meta-behavioral sciences. (The term "meta-science" has come into our vocabulary recently largely through the study of language. When we study a language we must be careful not to confuse the language which we are studying with the language by means of which we are studying it; the latter is commonly called a "meta-language.") Transferring the terminology, we may speak of certain disciplines as studies of sciences in much the same way that the sciences are studies of their own subject matter. Then meta-sociology (often called "social philosophy") will be one of the humanities; so also will be meta-economics, meta-political science, meta-education, and meta-psychology. The danger in this terminology is that a meta-science will be judged to be essentially the same kind of discipline as the science it studies. Nothing could be further from the truth. Meta-sciences are characterized by the fact that they examine the methods and presuppositions of the sciences which they study; they bring to light the assumptions; they clarify and validate the methods; and they evaluate the goals. Their methods may or may not be like the methods of the "lower level" sciences; usually they are quite different. C. D. Broad calls such studies "critical philosophy," and if he is correct all of the humanities are to this degree philosophical. Whether a study of any mode of behavior is one of the sciences or one of the humanities will depend upon the degree of critical analysis which is employed; this is difficult to decide in any case, but no more of a problem than it has been in the past when we have attempted to distinguish sociology from social philosophy, political science from political philosophy, or any other behavioral science from the examination of its methods and presuppositions.

Thus far we have seen that our map of the universe must contain abstractions, which are studied by mathematical logic; mass energy, which is studied by the physical sciences; life, which is studied by the biological sciences; and human valuational behavior, which is studied by the behavioral sciences. Furthermore, we have seen that each of these sciences may be pure or applied. And we have discovered that each applied science is potentially put to work to improve man's life on earth —a fact which generates a new category of "manipulators." These are roughly divided into two groups, not sharply differentiated from each other. On the one hand are those who make up the trades and professions; they pursue these activities as lifework. On the other hand, there are those of us who may or may not earn our living by these activities, but carry them on nevertheless either as avocations or attempts to fill out our individual lives in order to realize our full potentialities as human beings. Finally, there are the humanities or meta-sciences, whose subject matter and whose methods are quite different from any of those thus far considered. This, then, is our list of disciplines: mathematical logic, natural science (physical and biological), behavioral science, pure science, applied science, trades and occupations (which are not disciplines in the strict sense), and metascience. But this is not all.

For what I have just done is to draw a map of the universe, and such activity is not contained in any of the categories listed above. This is the task of the philosopher *par excellence.* Snow did not consider it important because he felt that it would lead to unnecessary subtleties. If these are all "cultures," then there are nine "cultures," not two. And the problems of the interrelations between them—which was his main consideration—are tremendously more complex than he had supposed. I have merely *listed* the disciplines; the task of *uncovering their complex interrelationships* is forbidding in its scope and intricacy. The purpose of this paper has been to discourage Snow from taking a third look. Without a map he will only sink deeper into the quagmires of "cultures."

NOTES

1. In the United States the lecture was published in hard covers (New York, 1959).
2. C. P. Snow, *The Two Cultures: and A Second Look* (Cambridge, England, 1964), p. 54.
3. *Ibid.,* p. 57. The work referred to was F. R. Leavis's *Two Cultures? The Significance of C. P. Snow* (first published, *Spectator* [March 9, 1962]; republished in hard covers, London, 1962).
4. Since the original essay is contained in this volume, I shall use its pagination for references to both essays, using the title, *Second Look.*
5. *Technology and the Academics* (New York, N.Y., 1959), p. 59.
6. *Second Look,* p. 54.
7. *Ibid.,* p. 55.
8. A striking example of the complex problems which arise in the use of this word is to be found in "Daedalus: Science and Culture," *Journal of the American Academy of Arts and Sciences* (Winter, 1965).
9. *Ibid.,* p. 62.
10. *Ibid.,* p. 64.
11. An attempt on the part of D. C. Beardslee and D. D. O'Dowd in an article entitled, "The College Student Image of the Scientist" (*Science,* CXXXIII, No. 3457, 997-1001), to determine the characteristic cultural traits of the scientist drew the conclusion, somewhat surprising in character, that scientists generally have unattractive wives.
12. *The New Statesman and Nation* (Oct. 6, 1956), 413-14.
13. *Ibid.,* p. 413.
14. *Ibid.,* p. 413.
15. *Webster's Collegiate Dictionary,* 1958 ed.
16. *Loc. cit.,* p. 413.
17. *Science,* CXLIII, No. 3601, 33.
18. *Second Look,* p. 65.
19. *Ibid.,* pp. 69-70.

20. Sir Eric Ashby (*op. cit.*) points out that this is much less true today (1959) than it was formerly.
21. Case Institute of Technology.
22. In at least two of Snow's earlier writings he emphasized the distinction strongly. See "The Enjoyment of Science", *Spectator,* CLVI (June 12, 1936), 1074-1075; and "What We Need from Applied Science," *Spectator,* CLVII (Nov. 20, 1936), 904.
23. *Second Look,* p. 61.
24. See A. Cornelius Benjamin, *Science, Technology and Human Values* (Columbia, Missouri, 1965).

PHILOSOPHY AND COMMON SENSE

by George Boas

I should no doubt begin by defining what I mean by the two nouns in the title of this paper. But were I to do so, I should need a book rather than an essay in which to explain what I am talking about. For it is a tradition in philosophy to push matters back to their logical beginnings and that would be impossible within any reasonable number of words. Assuming then that we know what we are talking about—an admittedly shaky assumption—let me say that my purpose here is to suggest how philosophy is sometimes guided by common sense and how sometimes common sense is guided by philosophy.

We all grow up with a set of ideas, logical principles, rules for thinking, whose origin is more or less obscure. We do not invent our language but inherit it from others. But language, as is granted by almost everyone nowadays, is itself a sort of philosophy, concealing or expressing, according to one's views, a peculiar metaphysics. Professors of literature are accustomed to studying the special figures of speech which dominate certain writers and sometimes these figures of speech are common to a literary era. The lark that mounts to Heaven's gate is no invention of Shakespeare's nor are the twin pools which stand for eyes. But the prevalence of figures of speech need not be sought in literature. We all know how certain slang expressions arise, extend themselves through a social class, and then fade away. We also know how certain words come into fashion and then go out of fashion. I doubt very much whether such fashions express anything whatsoever beyond the desire for social conformity. One gains the esteem of one's social group by doing what they do, wearing the same kind of clothes as they wear, attending the same lectures, reading the same books, playing the same games, and naturally enough speaking the same speech. So at times certain types of philosophical problem come into fashion, at the present logical, linguistic, and aesthetic. As far as I know, no one is studying the problems of God, freedom, and immortality, which were of such importance to Kant. "No one" in this context means "very few," for there is always a survival from past eras which remains to plague the generalizer in cultural history. It is safe to say that historians of philosophy have become almost extinct, though there are still a few specimens left, about as many as there are of whooping cranes.

Linguistic style, if it is symptomatic of anything, indicates a state of mind, not a set of ideas in the sense that declarative sentences may be said to express ideas. But at the same time most of us do submit to the almost universal syntactical rules of the language which we are trying to speak and it is here that some writers have imagined that they could unearth a concealed philosophy. Thus in English and, as far as I know, in all Indo-European languages, we use common nouns and adjectives. These are obviously symbols for classes of things and events, not for individuals. They obviously select groups of beings and do not differentiate the members of the groups from one another. Moreover, in modern languages nouns and adjectives have no tenses, though in some Amerindian languages they do. When we say the noun *house,* we leave out all reference to when it existed or exists or will exist, and if we wish for some reason or other to bring in dates, we have to do so either by using a peculiar tense of the verb or by some adverbial phrase. We distinguish in this way between the temporal series and that which takes place in it, as we say. We do not integrate time into the being of things. This, I hope, is obvious.

Moreover, our common nouns and adjectives specify no location in space. And when we wish to indicate spatial situations, we again have to resort to adverbial qualifiers. In Japanese one says this-here-house, that-there-house, and that-house-way-over-there. But in English we talk as if the things of which we are speaking were unconditioned by their whereabouts or their dates, a house or a dog being just as domiciliary or canine wherever they may be found. Yet one classical theory of epistemology, that based on sensory data, overlooks the indisputable fact that location in time and space determines what one will perceive, even, in the case of vision, the traditional source of sensory data, determining size and shape. In this way by reflecting upon our language, at least upon one kind of language, we discover that we speak as if we believed that there are certain beings which are inherently spaceless and timeless. There is surely no need here to do more than say that the universals embodied in language are without individuality, though with specificity. They are related to particular things in time and space in a way that has never been satisfactorily explained except in the eyes of the explainer.

If it were possible to have a language in which all the words were particularized, so that one could not speak of a dog or a house, but only of, let us say, my-house-here-and-now, and if each of the verbal symbols were as different from what they are in English as the symbols, *Abraham Lincoln* or *George Washington* are different, then there could be no problem of universals since there would be no universals whatsoever. We do have a language which is composed exclusively of general terms, the language of mathematics, and I am told that very primitive languages are much more particularized than ours. If the symbol for my-yesterday-knife and my-today-knife do not both include the symbol for knife, there is little likelihood of anyone's abstracting either from the objects in question or from the perception of those objects any common property. But that does not mean that a person speaking such a language would not know what a knife was. In an antithetical case we use one word *address* both for the name of where one lives and for a speech, but we seldom, if ever, confuse the two. So, though we still differentiate amongst babies, adolescents, and adults, we nevertheless can recognize the personal identity of a human being at his various periods of life. The problem of universals does not arise in mathematics until someone tries to apply it within limits to the spatiotemporal world. The problem arises right out of the conflict between what we call experience and universals and what I am calling here common sense.

Common sense sets the problem here because we see a discrepancy between its data and those of theory. We are living in space and time and suddenly become aware of beings that do not appear to be spatiotemporal. We are confronted with particulars and suddenly discover that they exemplify in some mysterious manner universals. And if we say, as some philosophers have said, that we are also confronted with universals and actually come face to face with the nonspatial and nontemporal here and there and, it goes without saying, at precise moments of time, then we have to explain how a timeless being can intrude into the world of time and not take on a date. For such intrusions occur at certain moments. And if we say that universals are only words, then we have to explain why particulars obey the dictates of those words. We can call things anything we please, but whether we call something by a great variety of names or not, we have to recognize it as having certain persistent traits which it shares with other things. And our old problem is before us again. For how are we to describe the sharing of common properties without involving universals?

We are thus in the position of granting that here a philosophic problem arises out of common sense. But we also have to grant that we shall not be satisfied with any solution of the problem which cannot be verified by common sense. But if in considering the rise of the problem we mean linguistic usage by common sense, we surely do not mean that when we are talking of verification. If we are talking about linguistic usage, then clearly there is caninity as well as dogs. But though it may be argued that the problem of the reality of universals arises because we use such a word as "caninity," and define it in general terms, it is not solved by pointing to the word. Before we can answer this question we have to have criteria of reality and those criteria are not to be found in grammars and dictionaries. It is not in a course in English Composition that one learns that dreams, hallucinations, optical illusions, ghosts, and negative afterimages are unreal. Nor is it through any experience of this set of unrealities. We discover that something perceived is unreal by comparing it with something that is real, not by simply looking at it. For no experience by itself, isolated from the total mass of our memories, ever says anything about its own reality. Judgments of reality are made after the event. One has to stop to think before passing on the reality of any experience. Our illusions would not mislead us if they announced their illusory nature as soon as they appeared before us. It is because we already know so much that we are seldom misled by the common illusions of perception. No one by experience uncorrected by thinking could have announced that the earth moves round the sun. If then we say that the sun is really stationary, it is not because of simple visual experience. We are constantly correcting our experience by means of what we know of science and philosophy.

One set of these criteria is certainly reflected in and stimulated by language. I refer to our growing use of abstractions that accompanies step by step the spread of natural science. What has been called the science of envelops is an example of this. The word "envelop" is used to name those more inclusive terms that have to be used as, for instance, biology is absorbed into chemistry, chemistry into physics, physics into mathematics. But science also has evolved in the direction of more inclusive or general laws. The stock example of this is physics, which up to the time of Newton had two sets of laws, one for sublunary and another for superlunary motions. But similarly in chemistry, until 1828 when urea was synthesized, there had to be two sets of laws, one for inorganic and another for organic substance. If then the name of a thing is made to connote its most general traits, those which it shares with other things, scientific names will become as abstract as nonscientific and for the purposes of science such abstractions may become essential.

For when it is of interest to make deductions, one has to have general propositions. In logic it is a case of all or none; in science it may be a case of most or almost none. In order to attain generalities, one has obviously to overlook those traits which distinguish one thing from another, and hence one has to develop techniques for overlooking them. These techniques are those of the laboratory. Fortunately for the philosopher, laboratory conditions are set up deliberately and for stateable purposes; they do not simply occur. And most scientific laws, when accurately phrased, include the conditions under which they are true. If I am not being too cynical, I should say that laboratory conditions are the conditions under which scientific laws become true. Moreover, when an event of a recognizable type occurs outside of a laboratory, such as a brick falling off a roof, a scientist is supposed to be able to explain why the law is not strictly obeyed. His explanation consists in measuring the difference between laboratory and nonlaboratory conditions. As primitive observers we first see each object as an individual thing and our classifications are originally made by our parents, siblings, and friends. We learn what to call things, what their names are, and presumably these names were applied because certain characteristics were selected as most important. Why they were important is now undiscoverable, though sometimes one's imagination helps. We can perhaps discover why children call railroad trains choo-choos and dogs bow-wows. We can also imagine that things that are irrelevant to the interests and knowledge of daily life are all lumped together, as children lump all numbers over a few as "a lot." When scientists first classified material objects as earthy, aerial, aqueous, and fiery, we no longer know what was their motive. But it must have taken a tremendous expansion of the scientific imagination to think of all substances as combinations of four. And a similar expansion of the imagination must have been required for Aristotle to reduce the complexity still further by making heat and moisture primary, defining cold and dryness as the simple absence of their opposites. The theory of the four elements, which gave rise to one of the most harmonious and general of theories, lasted well into the eighteenth century and was a triumph of science and philosophy over common sense. But it too had to meet the challenge of common sense. Experience, whatever its high status in empirical philosophies, is always a challenge to a philosopher for it refuses to behave as philosophers say it should. The discrepancies between common sense observation and scientific theory always exist and there is no rule that has as yet been formulated for telling a man when he must correct one by the other.

Sometimes philosophy corrects common sense instead of subjecting itself to it. But again we have to ask in what the correction consists. No one can deny the data of the visual world. They are simply there and, though we can explain them, we cannot explain them away. The correction must not be of the type which attributes them to a diseased mind. And I think I am right in saying that it first consists in accepting the tangible and ponderable object as the real one and then showing the conditions under which it will change its visual shape and size. I have been told by physicists that one could start with visual objects as real and interpret the behavior of tangible and ponderable ones as deviations from the visual norm. But I have also been told that such a system would become too complicated to be tolerated. If this is so, the criterion of simplicity is of primordial importance and should be examined. When Osiander says, in his introduction to Copernicus' *Revolutions of the Heavenly Spheres,* that nature always follows the simplest course, he means apparently a course that can be described with as few presuppositions and indefinables as possible. If one can define an event as a function of two variables, one has discovered something simpler presumably than a course that can be defined only in terms of three variables. But who can deny that the simplicity herein is not so much nature's as ours? Again, when Locke defined the real objects of the world in terms of those properties which were sufficient, if not necessary, for the construction of Galilean physics, he too simplified nature in the sense of reducing the number of its properties and correlating all other observable properties with change in human observation. But Locke thought he knew that the mind could know only ideas and that knowledge was the organization of ideas. And since he flatly refused to examine the mechanism by which ideas arose in the mind, but limited himself to studying the ideas after they had arisen, he was able to avoid many of the puzzles which his successors became mired in.

If common sense were to intervene at this point, it would observe that by this act of Locke's, at least three levels of beings were established: (1) the level of the Galilean properties; (2) the level of sensory qualities; and (3) the level of images, hallucinations, dreams, and illusions. These levels seem to be established by the degree of commonness of what is perceived: the Galilean properties are available to all observers under definable conditions; the secondary qualities are detectible only when a human mind is one of the variables of which they are functions; the third level is observable only to a single person at a time. Students who have taken even elementary courses in the history of philosophy will remember how Berkeley and Hume reduced these levels to one. That one was what Hume called the shifting theater of perception, in which there was no reason to believe either in a perceiving mind or in any causal relations in the ordinary sense of that term. As far as I know, the reasoning to this position was accurate, granting the presuppositions, and if Hume had carried it on to what we—who have the advantage of living two centuries later than he—would call its logical conclusion, he would have ended with that purely theoretical philosophy known as the solipsism of the present moment.

The strange thing about this conclusion is that when we have reached it, as Santayana did in the first part of *Scepticism and Animal Faith,* we immediately try to escape from it. We have a curious and perhaps unjustified feeling that though logically sound, there must be something wrong with it. We ask how we can prove the existence of other people's minds, of the past and the future, of the wall behind our backs, of the chair in the room next door. Nor does it occur to us that if the position is sound, such questions ought not even to occur to us. Why should we have this curious feeling? In fact, we might even ask how we could say that only I exist at this moment, if we did not believe that there were other minds to be distinguished from ours, other times from which the present is set off? This feeling is surely not the result of any theoretical considerations; it comes straight out of common sense. Moreover, one can hardly avoid asking the source of the rules by which we reach this apparently unsatisfactory conclusion. If we engage in extrapolations of our present experience into the past and future and other regions of space, where does the technique of extrapolation itself come from? Surely not from immediate observation. When one sees a patch of red, one does not and cannot deny that he sees it. He raises questions about it only when he tries to say something about it which goes beyond its redness. But why should he feel constrained to go beyond its redness, if only to ask what it is that is red? Only, I suggest, because one of the undeniable and persistent traits of our experience, whether perceptual or not, is its temporal dimension. We can no more divest ourselves of what common sense calls our memory than we can of the colors, sounds, tastes, and textures that arise before us.

Philosophers are rational people who work themselves into corners, not by committing fallacies, but by avoiding them; that can be said in their praise. But once they have got themselves into a corner, they seem unwilling to remain there and look for all sorts of devices by means of which they can escape. This is quite unlike what other rational people usually do. When we are told, for instance, that white light is a combination of all the spectral colors, absurd as this seems to common sense, we accept it as true. And when we are told that solid objects consist largely of empty space, we swallow that also and do not try to prove that empty space is really full. When we see great oaks from little acorns growing, we may wonder how it is possible, but we do not deny its possibility. And if someone were to maintain that great oaks could also grow from gloxinia seeds, and proved it by rigidly controlled experiments, repeating them in the traditional way, botanists would have to sigh and admit that it was true. Only intellectual Tories would insist that in reality the acorn was the real oak seed and that the oaks which grew out of the gloxinia seeds were illusions. It must not be denied that such intellectual Tories have existed—the history of the Copernican theory, of evolutionism, of the mechanical theory of heat, of indeed almost all scientific theories is evidence enough of the reluctance of the human race to accept the evidence for novelty. But sooner or later, unless such theories are disproved, and let us omit a discussion of what the disproof of a scientific theory consists in, they win out and are taught in textbooks as commonly accepted opinions. But no one to speak of ever accepted solipsism seriously in spite of the fact that no one could find a flaw in the argument leading to it.

When philosophers like Santayana introduce something called animal faith as a basis for our belief in those things for which we have no rational evidence, they say no more than if they had simply introduced common sense. Of course we believe in other people's minds, the room next door, a world of external objects, and all the rest. Without indulging in any intellectual tricks, let me say that whether one calls this kind of belief common sense or not, is a matter of indifference. What is not a matter of indifference is that there exists a set of beliefs which we have to justify and that it is not a set which we reach through demonstration, reasoning, experimentation, or revelation. This set of beliefs can be phrased as a set of propositions which do not demand proof and which act as the criteria of satisfactory theorizing. By this I mean that I do not have to prove the existence of the past or of the other things of whose existence certain epistemological theories raise doubts, unless we have already reached the conclusions that they do not exist. If I conclude that there is no past or no external world, I have the choice of going no further or of going back and trying to discover where my reasoning went astray. But the suspicion that my reasoning did go astray is what is of interest. It could not have happened because of the train of thought which led to the unsatisfactory conclusions, for if it had, I might have caught it in the act. I have obviously accepted a set of ideas as standard truths and use them to check my reasoning. We might be expected to say in philosophy that if we come out with no external world, no past, no future, no distant space, and so on, we have either committed an error in reasoning or that common sense has been in error. No proof is needed that frequently common sense has indeed been erroneous. To common sense the earth is flat, the sun moves through the skies from east to west, the moon waxes and wanes, and eels are generated from horsehairs. It might be expected to be wrong here too.

There are only two ways of critically examining an argument. One is to look at the premises and see whether they are acceptable or not; the other to look at the reasoning and see whether it is fallacious. I am assuming here, with most of my colleagues, that the reasoning of the solipsist is correct. We must therefore turn to the premises. And if the conclusions are to be tested by their harmony with common sense, then it might be expected that the premises would be similarly tested. If we want to prove that there is a room next door, we had best choose premises which will not make it impossible to do so. Among those premises must be the criteria by means of which we can tell whether a room exists or not. If we want to know what flag is flying from the mast of a ship, we must know what certain flags look like before we guess. And we must know this before we make our guess. That knowledge could not possibly arise out of the immediate data of sense. But if we grant this, we have to grant also that knowledge or, if you prefer, belief, has a history in everyman's biography.

Questions of this sort often arise because of the discrepancy between what we are seeing and what we expected to see. If we see a ship with the flag flying upside down, we cannot tell what it signifies unless we know the code. And I venture to say that it is not the sight of the flag upside down that raises the question in our minds but the expectation that it ought to be flying rightside up. The perceptual data in themselves are utterly inarticulate until they have been interpolated into a larger set of data which have been previously interpreted or given conventional significance. They are made to "say" something when their appearance can be inferred from other things as a rule, but no rule can be established on the single occurrence of any set of data, however complicated. There must be a long series of repeated events for the establishment of rules and no one can be confident that he has the right rule unless his experience is corroborated by that of other people. For just as our language assumes the existence of time and of other people's minds, so do our processes of verification.

The question of whether the sensory data are subjective or objective is irrelevant to the truth of knowledge in the sense of judgment. All that is required is that they occur in a regular and predictable manner. All that the scientific investigations of their origin proves is that they are functions of two variables: material stimuli, causes, sources, what you will, in the nonhuman world, and the whole perceptual apparatus of human beings. Neither alone will suffice. But if we are talking about knowledge in the sense of assertions or judgments, the sensory data become both the criteria of truth and error, and also the stimuli to questions. But both as criteria and as stimuli to questions, they are just dumb things when isolated from human interests. A single color, red, may be evidence of a large variety of statements and similarly a combination of sensory data may be required to prove a single simple statement. It takes but a few moments' reflection to show that there is no possibility of making a one-to-one correspondence between sensory data and all possible judgments.

To save space I shall say nothing of certain other metaphysical aspects of Indo-European languages, such as those involved in the subject-predicate proposition, the necessity of subjects for verbs, and the reification of processes. It is more important to emphasize something which is not inherently linguistic, the social element in knowledge. We demand that all truths be interpersonal. Just as we assume that anyone with the proper training can repeat someone else's experiments, and that no experiment can be accepted until it has been repeated, so we assume that any belief must be corroborated by others if we are to accept it. That there is such a thing as what used to be called an inner life is no doubt true, but it is of little use so long as it cannot be communicated. Such experiences as religious conversions, the beatific vision, the delusions of the mentally diseased, are of course experienced by only one person at a time. They clearly are no more interpersonal than a toothache. But what should concern the philosopher is not so much their privacy as the need their possessors feel of telling other people about them. The writing of lyric poetry, for instance, has the paradoxical factor of exteriorizing, as the French say, that which is internal. The situation suggests that we do not trust our own direct experience until it is shared by another. The anguish which is felt when the attempt at communication fails to reach its end is characteristic of the situation. It is as if one felt that experience must be shared or remain illusory. Thus common sense assumes without question not only the existence of other minds, but their function as witnesses to the truth of anybody's opinions.

I make no claim to having done anything more than state a problem. Common sense creates problems for the philosopher and also answers them. The many mansions of religion will have to be granted a place in philosophy as well. But to the man whom this volume is supposed to honor, this will not prove embarrassing.

CONSCIENCE AND CONSCIENTIOUSNESS

by A. Campbell Garnett

Professor Nowell-Smith tells a story of an Oxford don who thought it his duty to attend Common Room, and did so conscientiously, though his presence was a source of acute distress both to himself and others. This story is told in illustration of a discussion of the question whether conscientiousness is good without qualification. The philosopher's comment is "He would have done better to stay at home," and he reinforces this view with the historical judgment that "Robespierre would have been a better man (quite apart from the question of the harm he did) if he had given his conscience a thorough rest and indulged his taste for roses and sentimental verse."[1] The harm, in these cases, he points out, seems to spring, in part at least, from the very conscientiousness of these people, and he concludes that we have no reason for accepting the principle of the supreme value of conscientiousness and that there is nothing either self-contradictory or even logically odd in the assertion "You think that you ought to do A, but you would be a better man if you did B."[2]

This judgment, it should be noted, is a *moral* evaluation. "Better man" here means "ethically better." It explicitly excludes "better" in the sense of "more useful or less harmful to society" in the reference to Robespierre. Further, it is not restricted to the mere right or wrong of overt acts, saying, for example, that Robespierre would have done less that is objectively wrong if he had attended to his roses more and his conscience less, for it is a judgment on the moral character of the *man,* not merely on that of his overt acts, and moral judgments upon a man must take account of every feature of his personality concerned in the performance of his acts, i.e., his motives, intentions, character, beliefs, abilities and so forth. What we have here, therefore, is the contention that in some cases where conscientiousness would lead to more harm than good (as it may do in cases of mistaken moral judgments or other ignorance) a man may be a morally better man by stifling his conscience and doing what he believes he ought not to do. It is not claimed that this will always be true in such cases, and it is not denied that conscientiousness is to some degree a value. But it is denied that it is the only moral value, or a value with supreme authority above all others, or that it is an essential feature of all moral value.

These denials are not uncommon among contemporary moralists, but it should be noted that they constitute a rejection of the major tradition in moral philosophy, from Plato to the present day. They also conflict with the convictions of the common man expressed in such injunctions as "Let your conscience be your guide," "Do what you yourself believe to be right, not what others tell you," "Act on your own convictions," "Always act in accord with your own conscience," "To thine own self be true." Conscientiousness is firmness of purpose in seeking to do what is right, and to most people it seems to be the very essence of the moral life and a value or virtue in some sense "higher" or more important than any other. Among philosophers this view is notably expressed in Joseph Butler's doctrine of the "natural supremacy" of conscience and in Immanuel Kant's insistence that there is nothing good in itself, intrinsically good, save the good will, and that this consists in the will to do one's duty for duty's sake. There are, evidently, some complex issues and confusions involved in these sharply varying positions and to clarify them we shall need to begin with an examination of what is involved in conscience itself.

Analysis of Conscience

Conscience involves both a cognitive and an emotive or motivational element. The cognitive element consists in a set of moral judgments concerning the right or wrong of certain kinds of action or rules of conduct, however these have been formed. The emotive or motivational element consists of a tendency to experience emotions of a unique sort of approval of the doing of what is believed to be right and a similarly unique sort of disapproval of the doing of what is believed to be wrong. These feeling states, it is generally recognized, are noticeably different from those of mere liking or disliking and also from feelings of aesthetic approval and disapproval (or aesthetic appreciation) and from feelings of admiration and the reverse aroused by nonmoral activities and skills. They can become particularly acute, moving and even distressing, in the negative and reflexive form of moral disapproval of one's own actions and motives, the sense of guilt and shame. In this form (indeed in both forms) they may have some notably irrational manifestations, but the sense of shame also has a very valuable function as an inhibitory motive upon the person who contemplates the possibility of doing what he believes to be wrong.

These are the commonly recognized aspects of conscience, and they frequently function quite uncritically. Because of this uncritical emotive reaction conscience all too frequently moves people to approve or disapprove actions and rules concerning which adequate reflection would lead to a very different verdict, and sometimes it afflicts people with a quite irrational sense of guilt. These deplorable effects of some manifestations of conscience are a large part of the reason for its devaluation in the judgment of many modern moralists. What these thinkers rightly deplore is the uncritical emotive reaction which the person who experiences it calls his conscience, particularly when the emotive element in it inhibits any critical activity of the cognitive element. But it is not necessary, and it is not usually the case, that the emotive element in conscience stifles the critical, and there is no justification for jumping to the conclusion that conscience should be ignored. For critical ethical thinking is itself usually conscientiousness, and conscience can be trained to be habitually critical.

For clarity of thinking on this question we need to distinguish between the critical and the traditional conscience. The latter is uncritical. Here the emotive element attaches to moral ideas accepted from the tradition without critical re-evaluation of them. Its strength lies in this perpetuation of tradition, but this is also the source of its errors. It is this blind but emotive perpetuation of an outgrown and mistaken condition that contemporary critics of the supreme evaluation of conscience, for the most part, are concerned to deplore. And thus far they are right. But one would be unfair to such critics if one were not to recognize that their efforts to point out the errors of the tradition are usually also conscientious and are not merely the echoing of another tradition. Sometimes their critical ideas are boldly new and very commonly they are presented with persistent and painstaking care and in spite of personal cost. Nietzsche and Marx, Schweitzer and Gandhi, as well as Robespierre, were thoroughly conscientious men. Their ideas were new but were held with great emotive strength and tenacity. The same is true of the prophets of Israel and the great moral innovators of other religions. Indeed, the outstanding examples of conscientious men are not the mere sustainers of a tradition but the thinkers who try to improve the tradition.

This fact of the vitality of the critical conscience shows the superficiality of Freud's identification of it with the superego and of the explanation of it as an aftereffect of early social conditioning, as put forward by many psychologists and sociologists, and uncritically adopted by many philosophers. On this view the moral judgments which tend to arouse spontaneous emotions of approval or disapproval, shame and guilt, are those which we learned to make in our childhood and which we then heard expressed by those around us accompanied by strong manifestations of moral approval and disapproval. The child, it is pointed out, must naturally assimilate the tendency to feel similar emotions whenever he himself makes a moral judgment, and this emotive tendency remains with him in adult life together with the tendency to frame and express such judgments. Conscience is then said to be simply the inward echo of the emotionally expressed judgments of our childhood social environment. This may be accepted as part of the explanation of the emotive element in the uncritical traditional conscience, but as an explanation of how men come to feel the way they do about the results of their own original critical thinking, and of the motivational drive conscientiously to do original critical ethical thinking, it is woefully inadequate.

It is not difficult to see how the cognitive element in conscience, the judgment of right and wrong, becomes critical. To some extent it must be so from the beginning. A favorite word in every child's vocabulary is "Why?" And especially does he ask for reasons when told that he *ought* to do something he does not want to do. If moral injunctions are accepted as such on mere authority it is because it is implicitly believed that the authority *has* good reasons for issuing them, or else that the demand or example of this authority is in itself a sufficient reason for obedience or conformity, as with kings and deities. Apart from authority, reasons for moral rules have to be found in their relevance to the needs and security and peace of the community and the well-being of the person himself. But always, it is a distinguishing mark of a *moral* rule that it is one for which it is believed that reasons can be given. Critical thinking about moral rules is therefore stimulated whenever the reasons presented seem inadequate, beginning with the child's "Why?" and whenever there is a conflict of rules.

This critical thinking at first accepts as its basic principles the sort of reasons customarily given for moral rules and injunctions—the traditions of the tribe, its peace, security, prosperity and honor, revelations from divine sources, and so forth. But at a higher level of critical thinking conflicts are found between these basic principles themselves, and man is directed to the philosophical task of thinking out the *most* basic of all principles—if any such can be found. The search may end in scepticism and confusion, but so long as the thinker is prepared to accept any reason at all as a reason why something "ought" (in the ethical sense) to be done he is also convinced that he ought to do that which his search for reasons has led him to believe that he ought to do. Further, the experience of finding reasons for rejecting old views and accepting new ones impresses upon him the need and value of the search. Thus, so long as he recognizes any moral reasons at all he must recognize a duty of continued critical examination of moral ideas. The critical conscience thus becomes its own stimulus to further critical thinking. Conscience takes the form of the firm conviction, not merely that one ought to do what one believes one ought to do, still less that one ought to do without question what one has been taught one ought to do, but that one ought to think for oneself as to what one really ought to do and then act on one's own convictions. And the emotive drive is apt to attach itself as firmly to this last formulation of the cognitive element in conscience as ever it does to the other two.

Conscience, Love and Personal Integrity

It is clear that the motivational element of conscience in its most developed form is not merely the continuing echo of approvals and disapprovals of specific rules and actions impressed upon us by the social environment of our childhood. Yet the emotive content is continuous through all the changes in the sort of action the contemplation of which arouses it. One can imagine a youth of the eighteenth century feeling strong moral approval of a man who challenges a dangerous opponent to a duel in defense of his wife's good name, and later, in his maturity, feeling similar moral approval of another man who faces social obloquy for his refusal to fight a duel in similar circumstances because he is opposed in principle to duelling. In both cases it is the manifestation of courage in defense of principle that calls forth the moral approval, but his judgment has changed as to the mode of action appropriate to such defense. We see that what has changed is the specific sort of action that calls forth approval and disapproval, while what remains the same is the specific sort of reason that is held to be appropriate for judging an action to be worthy of approval or disapproval. And this we would find to be true in general (if we had space to demonstrate it) through the whole process of critical re-examination of moral judgment. Moral approval and disapproval attach to whatever we find to have reasons for approval. These reasons, in the course of thinking, become more and more specifically formulated and more and more highly generalized into abstract principles of moral judgment and they are only changed as change is seen to be needed to bring them into consistency with one another. Emotive unwillingness to accept some of the consequences of this process of ethical thinking sometimes inhibits and distorts it, but through it all the emotive drives of approval and disapproval tend to attach themselves to whatever lines of action are thought to be characterized by the recognized reasons for such attitudes.

On account of the complexity of all their implications the exact and proper statement of these basic ethical principles is a matter of very great difficulty. Yet there is a degree of agreement as to general principle which is really remarkable considering the complexity of human conduct and the diversity of traditional moral judgment with which we start. Thus, there is almost universal agreement that the fact that an act may have bad consequences for some persons is a good reason for disapproving it, and the reverse if it would have good consequences. Similarly there are certain rules of justice that are generally recognized, such as that of impartiality in the distribution of goods and burdens, the keeping of contracts and promises, the making of reparations, and the equitable application of the law. Questions arise as to how far the duties of beneficence should go, as to what to do when principles conflict in practical application, as to whether all principles can be comprehended under some one principle, and so forth. But the general trend is clear. Moral approval and disapproval are moved by the thought of the effect of our actions upon the weal or woe of human beings. This is the root of conscience. If some conscientious thinkers, such as Nietzsche, seem to be an exception to this rule it is because they have developed unusual or paradoxical views of what really constitutes true human weal or woe, or how it can best be promoted.

This connection of conscience with reasons for action bearing on the effects of action on human well-being enables us to understand the distinctive feeling-tone of moral approval and disapproval—i.e., their difference from mere liking and disliking, and from other emotions such as the aesthetic, and from nonmoral admiration and its reverse. The moral emotions are often mingled with these others, but they are also different. There is in them a distinct element of concern for human welfare which is gratified by what promotes it and distressed at anything that seems injurious. For this reason the moral emotions have often been identified with sympathy, but they are not mere passive feeling states. There is in them an element of active concern for human values with an impulse to give help where it seems needed. For this reason these emotions are responsive to judgments about the effects of human action, bringing forth a positive response of approval to that which seems helpful and the reverse toward the hurtful. For this reason also moral approval is a gratifying emotion, inducing a favorable reaction, while moral disapproval is apt to become a source of distress and an occasion for anger. For moral approval, we can now see, is a specification in action of the most deeply satisfying of all human emotions, that of love, in its most general form of expression.

Moral approval, then, is a development of the basic social interest of man as a social animal, it is an expression of the general sympathetic tendency of concern for human values with special attention to those depending on the orderly life of the group. It is an expression of the desire to create and maintain those values. Its conflict with other motives is, therefore, a conflict of desires. But this particular conflict, the conflict of conscience (moral approvals and disapprovals) with other desires (temptations) is not just an ordinary conflict of desires. It is a conflict in which the integrity of the personality is peculiarly involved. In an ordinary conflict of desires, in which there is no moral issue, the best solution is for one of the desires to be completely set aside and fade into oblivion without regrets, the opposing interest being completely triumphant. And, for the integrity of the personality it does not matter which interest gives way. But if the conflict be between "conscience" (the interests involved in moral approval and disapproval) and "temptation" (some opposed interest or desire) then it does matter which triumphs. The integrity of personality is involved. It tends to dissolve as a person slips into the habit of doing things he believes to be wrong. He loses his self-respect and his firmness of purpose. For a time the sense of guilt depresses. Later it tends to be repressed. With these psychological repressions the personality tends to manifest either general weakness or the overcompensations which give a false impression of strength as they manifest themselves in irrational drives. The guilty conscience and the repressed conscience are at the root of most of the disorders of personality, whether the guilt itself be reasonably conceived or not.

It is evident, therefore, that the emotive or motivational element that manifests itself in conscience is rooted in conative tendencies or interests which are of basic importance in the life of man. This psychological conclusion has, in recent years, been strongly emphasized by a number of workers in the field of psychotherapy, notably by Erich Fromm, who argues strongly that only in what he calls the "orientation of productive love"[3] can the personality of man develop continuously and with the integrity necessary for mental health. From this conclusion concerning the psychological need of this type of orientation Fromm also develops a most important theory of conscience. What we have distinguished as the critical and uncritical (or traditional) conscience he distinguishes as the "authoritarian" and the "humanistic" conscience. The former he dismisses as the internalized voice of an external authority, but the latter, he maintains, is "the reaction of our total personality to its proper functioning or disfunctioning. . . . Conscience is thus . . . the voice of our true selves which summons us . . . to live productively, to develop fully and harmoniously. . . . It is the guardian of our integrity."[4]

If Fromm's psychological analysis of the growth and structure of personality is accurate in essentials, and if our account of the growth of the critical conscience out of the uncritical is also correct, then we must recognize that conscience at every stage is, as Fromm says of the "humanistic" conscience, "the reaction of our total personality to its total functioning," its "voice" is the experience of the constraint of the personality as a whole, in its seeking of a growing creative expression with integrity or wholeness, upon the occasional and temporary impulses and desires which would tend to stultify its creativity and destroy its integrity. It is because doing what we believe we ought not is destructive of that integrity that conscience demands that we always act in accord with our own convictions; and it is because the fundamental orientation of human life is social and creative that ethical thinking tends, through the course of history, to clarify itself in the light of principles which tend to formulate moral judgments as expressions of impartial concern for human well-being.

The Authority of Conscience

It is time now to return to the question with which we started. Is it true that a man would sometimes be a better man (i.e., morally better) for refusing to obey his conscience rather than obeying it? It should be noted that the question is not whether the consequences to himself or to others might be better in general, but whether he would, himself, be a morally better man for acting in this way. This raises the question whether it is ever morally right to go against one's conscience. Is it ever right to do as you think you ought not to do? And this, again, is not the question whether conscience is always right in what it commands us to do, but whether it is ever right to disobey those commands, thus choosing to do what we believe to be wrong? The traditional answer is given by Joseph Butler in asserting the "natural supremacy" of conscience, which "magisterially asserts itself and approves and condemns." "Had it strength as it had right: had it power, as it had manifest authority, it would absolutely govern the world."[5] Against this we have the contemporary challenge voiced by Nowell-Smith.

One serious objection to this modern challenge to the traditional view is that it is necessarily futile and worse than futile, as a guiding principle of moral behaviour. It is futile because, though a man may believe that *perhaps,* in some cases, it *may* be that he would be a better man if he did not do what he believes he ought to do, he can never believe this in any particular case, for that would be to believe that he ought not to do this that he believes he ought to do, which is self-contradictory. Thus this piece of ethical theory is so paradoxical that it can never function as a guide to action. Further, it is worse than futile, for it implies, not merely that moral judgment may be mistaken (and therefore needs critical examination) but that the very effort not to do wrong may itself sometimes be wrong—that the conscientious effort to try to find out what is really right and act firmly in accord with one's own convictions, is sometimes wrong and we have no way of knowing when it is wrong. From this state of mind the only reasonable reaction is to abandon the ethical inquiry and the ethical endeavor and make the easiest and most satisfactory adjustment we can to the mores of the community and the practical exigencies of our personal situation.

The logical alternatives, therefore, are either to abandon the moral standpoint entirely, or to affirm, with Butler, the moral authority of every man's own conscience. The fact that judgments conscientiously made may be in error does not imply that this assertion of the sovereignty of the individual conscience must lead to either conflict or chaos. It rather avoids conflict, for each person, in asserting the rights of his own conscience, at the same time affirms the right of freedom of conscience for others. And it avoids chaos because, laying the injunction upon us to exercise continuous critical examination of our own moral judgments, it points us on the only possible way to consistency and order in moral judgment, by finding our errors and rectifying them. A community of people open-mindedly seeking the best formulation and reformulation of its moral rules, and abiding by its most intelligent findings, is more likely to maintain order with progress than one in which conscience operates in any other way, or in no way at all.

We must conclude, then, that if one were to accept Nowell-Smith's critique of conscience one could not apply it to the decision of any moral question in one's own conduct, and that its acceptance, if taken seriously, would be apt to have a deteriorating effect upon personal moral endeavor. But it is still possible to grant it theoretical credence and apply it to our evaluation of the moral value of the personality of others. This is what Nowell-Smith does in the cases of Robespierre and the Oxford don: Robespierre would have been a better man if he had indulged his taste for roses and sentimental verse rather than follow the demands of his conscience that he strive by whatever terrible means seemed necessary to carry through the program of the revolution; and the Oxford don would have been a better man if he had allowed his personal distaste for Common Room society to overcome his sense of duty which required him to attend it.

This is a judgment on the moral quality of the man as affected by his act of choice. The choice with which we are concerned is not that of his decision as to whether A or B is the right thing to do but his decision as to whether he would do what he believed to be the right thing or follow his personal wishes to do something that he found much more agreeable to himself. The latter act is the one he would do if he had not given any consideration to the effect of his actions on other people, or the needs of the social structure of which he is a part, except so far as his own interests were involved, and, coming as it does after he has considered these things and formed a judgment as to what they require of him, it is a decision to set aside the results of this thoughtful examination of the possible consequences of his conduct and do the thing he personally wants to do and would have done if he had never given the matter any ethical thought at all. When the issue is thus clearly stated it is very difficult to see how any thoughtful person could judge the unconscientious following of inclination to be the act of a better man, or an act that tends to make a better man, than the careful thinking and active self-determination involved in conscientiousness. It seems evident that those who have expressed the view that the following of personal inclination is sometimes morally better than conscientiousness are confusing this issue with another to which we must next give attention.

Conscientiousness and Other Values

For Immanuel Kant there was nothing good in itself, good without qualification, except a good will, and a good will, he explains, is good, not because it is a will to produce some good, or even the greatest possible good, but simply by reason of the nature of its volition as a will to do one's duty, a will to do what is conceived as right. Thus, for Kant, an action only has *moral* worth if it is done from a sense of duty, not from any inclination, even that of an impartial desire to promote general human well-being. Kant does not deny that good-natured inclinations have value, but he insists that the will to do one's duty has incomparably higher value and that it alone is of distinctly moral value. Kant's position here is an extreme one. Conscientiousness is regarded not merely as an essential part of moral value but as the only truly moral value and supreme among all values. Against this Nowell-Smith is not alone in protesting, and it is this rejection of the extravagant claim for conscientiousness as compared with other values, that seems to him to justify the notion that there are some occasions when some other value should be preferred and conscientiousness rejected.[6]

It is true, as Nowell-Smith says, that "we normally think of moral worth as meaning the worth of any virtuous motive and we normally think of sympathy and benevolence as virtuous motives."[7] It is also true, that, contrary to Kant, we normally judge a right action done out of sympathy and good will to be morally better than the same action would be if done solely from a sense of duty but without sympathy or good will.[8] These normal judgments I think we must fully endorse, but they do not involve the implication that a man can be morally justified (i.e., can be a "better man" than he otherwise would be) in performing an act, even of sympathy and good will (let alone indulging an interest in roses), which, in the circumstances, he regards as wrong.

There is a story told by Mark Twain of two ladies who lied to protect a runaway slave even though believing it wrong to do so and fearing that they might suffer in hell for their sin. In such a case we see a conflict, not merely of conscience with desire, but of the uncritical or traditional conscience with the critical. The deeper level of conscience, which they might well have called their "intuitions," urged the protection of the poor, frightened slave. They were not sufficiently capable of philosophical thinking to formulate a philosophical critique in support of their own deeper insights, so they remained superficially of the traditional opinion that their action was wrong. But their choice was actually a conscientious one, true to the deeper levels of conscience, and we tend to endorse their decision because it is endorsed by our consciences too. But this example (and others like it) is not a case of judging that the motives of love and sympathy were here better than conscientiousness, but of judging that the will to do good, seen as the very root of righteousness, is better than the will to conform to rules uncritically accepted as right. Such a judgment is far from the same as judging that the Oxford don would have been a morally better man for indulging his reluctance to attend Common Room than he would for conscientiously fulfilling what he believed to be his duty in the matter.

If we accept a teleological ethics then we recognize that the purpose of moral rules is to protect and promote the more important aspects of social well-being. We then see that the motives of love and sympathy, if sufficiently strong, enlightened and impartial, would achieve the purposes of moral rules better than the moral rules do, and would also achieve other good purposes beyond them. A world of saints would be a better world than a world of conscientious persons without mutual love and sympathy. Seeing this, though there are no saints, we endorse such elements of saintliness as there are (i.e., love and sympathy expressed in this enlightened and impartial way) and recognize them as morally good and as expressions of a better type of personality than one in which conscientiousness is found without these motives. But this recognition of the greater value of enlightened and impartial good will, or love, can never involve a rejection of conscientiousness in favor of such love, for such love includes and transcends all that conscientiousness stands for. Such love is the fulfilling of the law and the fulfilling, not the rejection, of the conscientiousness which supports the law. Thus, while a teleological ethics rejects Kant's apotheosis of the will to do one's duty as the only intrinsic moral value it does not lead to an endorsement of the view that we should sometimes judge a man as morally better for neglecting his conscience to indulge some other inclination. If, on the other hand, we were to accept a deontological ethics we should find that to speak of a conflict between conscientiousness and an enlightened and impartial love and sympathy (or any other good motive) as a conflict between different moral values involves a category mistake. For conscientiousness and other good motives, on this view, are not moral values in the same sense. An act of love is not made moral by the kind of consequences at which it aims. The only moral actions are those which intentionally adhere to intuitively discerned principles. So whatever value is attached to love and sympathy, it is not moral value. Moral value belongs alone to conscientiousness. Thus a man could never become morally better by rejecting the morally valuable motive of conscientiousness for some other motive to which only nonmoral value is attached. This deontological theory Nowell-Smith, I think rightly, rejects, but it is well to see that it, too, involves a rejection of his theory of the comparison of conscientiousness with other moral values.

Returning to the teleological point of view, and reflecting on the deontologist's claim, we can perhaps see the reason for the basic confusions that haunt people's minds on this question of the relative value of conscientiousness and impartial good will, or love. Conscientiousness is uniquely a moral motive in that its end is morality itself, the keeping of moral rules. All other motives, if without conscientiousness, are at best nonmoral (operating without concern for moral rules) or at worst immoral—consciously in opposition to them. This is true even of love and sympathy, simply as such. But if the teleological point of view is correct it is not true of love and sympathy *with a concern for impartiality,* for this latter is the very basis of moral rules and such love is of the essence of the moral life. Thus conscientiousness and impartial good will share together the unique character of being moral in the sense of being motivated by a concern for morality as such, the former for the rules which formulate it in lines of conduct, and the latter for the basic principle of impartial concern for human well-being in accordance with which the rules merely formulate the guiding lines. But this merely means that impartial good will is a motive characterized by the critical conscience, while conscientiousness without love, sympathy or good will is an operation of the traditional or uncritical conscience alone. Thus the motive that is of uniquely moral value and of supreme moral authority is love finding expression in the form of the critical conscience.

The main conclusions, therefore, of this paper may be summed up briefly thus: (1) Conscientiousness, if it be properly critical, is good without qualification, but an uncritical conscientiousness is not. (2) Since we cannot be saints we need to be conscientious, and this includes both the effort to find out what we really ought to do and the effort to do it to the best of our ability. (3) We should also cultivate the motive of impartial love or good will, for it functions as both an illuminating guide and support to our efforts to be conscientious and is itself of intrinsic moral value. (4) We can be righteous, and to that extent good, men merely by being conscientious, but we can be much better men by being not only conscientious but men in whom, without conflicting with conscience, the effort to be conscientious is made unnecessary by the outflow of spontaneous good will. These are very ordinary conclusions, but it takes clear thinking to keep them free from some very extraordinary objections.

NOTES

1. P. H. Nowell-Smith, *Ethics* (London, 1954), p. 247.
2. *Ibid.,* p. 253.
3. Erich Fromm, *Man For Himself* (New York, 1947), pp. 92-107.
4. *Ibid.,* pp. 158-160.
5. Joseph Butler, *Five Sermons* (New York, 1950), p. 41.
6. Nowell-Smith, *op. cit.,* p. 245.
7. *Ibid.,* p. 246.
8. *Ibid.,* p. 259.

CRITERIA FOR IDEAS OF GOD

by Charles Hartshorne

Since Plato at least, philosophers have been trying to understand the idea of God. According to Plato himself, there is some reason to doubt the possibility of success in this undertaking. And, after 24 centuries, the whole matter seems still thoroughly controversial. Yet we cannot simply dismiss the question. Religious faith, of many kinds, and also unfaith, is still with us, and if philosophy is of no help in evaluating the various conceptions of deity, in what important matter is it likely to be helpful?

Evaluation implies criteria: by what criteria can conceptions of God be tested? There seem to be three possibilities: scientific tests, philosophic tests, and religious tests. The crucial scientific criterion seems to be in the yielding of successful predictions on as wide a scale as possible. Can ideas of God be tested by their predictive value? Here we must make a distinction. If someone says that God has decreed, and will infallibly bring to pass, a second coming of Christ within ten years, an event to be accompanied by certain definite, easily recognizable circumstances, then if the ten years pass and the predicted phenomena have not taken place, this particular idea about God will have been falsified. But note two things: (1) The failure of the prediction does not imply that God does not exist, for the decree which has been attributed to God is supposed to be his free decision, and all that one could conclude from the failure of the prophecy is that the prophet's idea of what God intends to bring about has turned out a bad guess. God apparently has other intentions. (2) The *essential* attributes to be attributed to deity are unaffected by the failure of the prediction. We cannot say, for instance, that since God has not arranged a second coming he must be lacking in goodness or wisdom. For to know what infinite wisdom must bring about in particular cases one would need to possess such wisdom oneself.

I believe that similar arguments will show that there is no way in which the predictive test could apply to the essential "attributes" of God, as distinct from his free decrees. Now it is these attributes which philosophy tries to ascertain. Anything beyond that is a matter for revelation, religious intuition, guesswork, or science. How, you may ask, can science enter into the picture? One way is this: it seems a reasonable view (supposing belief in God) that the laws of nature proceed from something like divine decrees. As we ascertain such laws we can, if we are believers, add to each law the interpretation, "thus has God decreed." For granting—as I would—that some freedom is allotted to the creatures, it seems unlikely that their freedom could go so far as to decide the very laws of nature. Even man seems entirely helpless to decide such laws (as objective regularities, rather than theoretical formulae aimed at their description). At most, man can discover the laws. Hence the believer may well see in natural laws or regularities manifestations of the divine will.

The believer cannot, in the same simple way, see the divine will in particular events, such as those of history, for here creaturely freedom plays its largest role; nor perhaps do we know any very definite laws of history. But, although natural laws do presumably express the divine will, they do not characterize God in his essential attributes unless we suppose, with Spinoza and the Stoics, that God, in instituting laws, acts entirely from the necessity of his nature and not from freedom. Could not God have decreed other laws, and still have been just as wise and good? No one can prove that the particular laws are better or worse than others which might have obtained in their place. It follows that science cannot test the correctness of our beliefs concerning the goodness or wisdom of deity. True enough, *for the believer,* the laws of nature "declare the glory of God, and the framework of things showeth his handiwork"; but they do not prove, and could not disprove, the validity of this belief. They illustrate its validity, but only *for* or *to* the believer, and hence cannot be used either to justify or to discredit his faith.

It is a common notion that the evil in the world furnishes a test of our view of the divine attributes, since it implies that either the goodness and wisdom, or the power, of God must be limited. I hold that this is incorrect. For any notion of divine power which, together with divine wisdom and goodness, seems to imply a world devoid of evil is a notion which will get us into trouble quite apart from the "problem of evil" or from any merely empirical problem. I reason as follows. If the perfection of power meant the ability to decide all events unilaterally, the exercise of this power would mean that the creatures made no genuine decisions at all. But this is doubly absurd, for (1) the creatures would then not even know what it is like to decide, and so they could not conceive divine decisions, and (2) how can the creatures, products of supreme freedom, have simply *no* freedom? Can the creatures, as effects, be *absolutely* different from their chief Cause?

If, for these reasons, the notion of a divine decision-making which left nothing for the creatures (any creatures, not just human beings) to decide is absurd, then—evil or no evil—we must conceive the "all-mighty" in such a way that the world is not in its details divinely decided, but is rather the result of the divine decisions *plus* innumerable creaturely decisions. But then no amount of evil could prove that God has decreed that evil, since creaturely freedom may account for all of it. Thus I conclude that the supposed empirical disproof of the divine attributes is spurious, since the ideas it is supposed to be capable of contradicting include at least one pseudo-conception with no clear and consistent meaning. We do not need observations to get rid of nonsense, but only clear thinking. I am convinced that any divine attribute which appears susceptible of empirical test will prove spurious in similar fashion.

Of course we can test the value for human beings of accepting this or that idea of God. We can compare the behavior of believers and nonbelievers, and see how well each meets certain standards. However, even supposing all difficulties as to the relevance and application of the standards, ethical or practical, can be met, the procedure will at best show nothing as to the existence or nonexistence of God—or as to his essential attributes. For, how far it is needful for man to consciously accept or know God is a question about *man's* essential nature, not God's. The lower animals cannot be conscious of God; man apparently can be, but apparently also he need not be. Are we able to decide how far a wise and good God would make it necessary, or even helpful, to such more or less "rational" animals as ourselves to reach agreement among themselves concerning their creator's existence and nature?

I conclude that there can be *no* empirical test of the correctness of the essentials of theistic beliefs. What tests then can there be? If there can be none, philosophy can at most serve to warn us against the vain attempt to apply rational considerations where they cannot be relevant. And then how would we deal with the situation? By sheer faith, or sheer unfaith? But there are many faiths; how should we choose among them? Again, by sheer faith, or lack of it? This seems a counsel of despair.

In mathematics and logic we have tests which are not empirical but intellectual—applications, in some sense, of "pure reason." Traditionally, philosophy has thought that to these should be added tests of metaphysical reasoning, called "dialectic" by Plato. However, today we face a great crisis in what is sometimes called metamathematics, and also in meta-metaphysics—in other words, in the theory of knowledge a priori or by reason alone. There is a strong tendency to attenuate such knowledge, trivialize it, by reducing it to a mere matter of the rules of our language, or the like. In knowledge by pure reason we are, it is thought, only reminding ourselves of our own communication needs and goals. Thus in the end we come down indirectly to something empirical or contingent after all. This paradox, upheld by Wittgenstein, Quine, and Goodman, among others, but only partially or not at all accepted by other leading logicians, including Popper, Lewis, Whitehead, Peirce, Scholz, Bochensky, Martin, and others, has made it extremely difficult to deal with the theistic question.

It is plain to all that mere deduction alone can tell us only that certain premises entail certain conclusions. And this means that knowledge as to what exists that is achieved by deduction alone can never be more than hypothetical. Thus if to be human is to be mortal and if there are men, then there are some mortal things; but the conclusion is not guaranteed by mere deduction.

Even the ontological proof for the divine existence is hypothetical, so far as the merely deductive part is concerned, and this is clear enough in Anselm's own statements. For one premise of the proof is that even the fool can "conceive" God, meaning, he can have a definite and self-consistent idea of him. Or as Leibniz put it: from the logical *possibility* of the divine existence, the existence itself may be deduced. But the possibility is not deduced; rather, it is assumed. (In another argument Anselm also attempts to deduce the possibility, but only by further assumptions not then and there deduced.) Always something is taken as otherwise known, if existence is to be proved. This seems to apply even to mathematical "existence." Deduction presupposes "intuition" into truth, if it is to lead to further truth.

Suppose we grant this, does it follow that all knowledge of existence comes around to *empirical* intuition, observation of mere matters of fact? This is the key question. My answer is in the negative. But to defend this answer is not especially easy.

We know as an historical fact that those who have accepted the ontological argument have tended to assert some version of the Augustinian doctrine of "illuminationism," the view that we have intuitive participation in the divine Light, the divine existence itself. According to this doctrine, the idea of God makes sense for us partly because, in a fashion, we know God himself even in barely thinking him. We can seek him only because we have never entirely lost him. I hold an epistemology from which it follows deductively that *either* God is impossible *or* he not only exists but exists as datum of *every* experience. Hence, even in rejecting the divine impossibility, I am, in my own view, affirming an intuition of God as inherent in all experience. This obligates no one who fails to find such an intuition in his own consciousness. But my proposition is this: those who deny being aware of God can, if they are willing to pursue the inquiry to the end, be led into difficulties deducible from this denial, whereas the assertion that we do experience God (properly conceived—we are coming to that) leads to no comparable difficulties. The difficulties in question are not conflicts with empirical facts, but mutual conflicts among meanings or purposes. By these conflicts the professed unbeliever betrays his internal disharmony, a disharmony which must arise if it be true that all are bound to experience God.

Is this an argument from a contingent fact? No, for the point is not that we happen in fact to experience God, but that, on the view I am asserting, an experience of which God is not a datum is impossible. Not simply *this* world as experienced requires God to explain it; but *any* experienceable world whatever, and any conceivable absence of a world, would equally require God. Thus to experience or think at all is to experience or think God, though not necessarily to do so consciously. Any world must be God's world, and any lack of a world must be God's lack of a world. The term "God" stands either for the principle of all meaning whatsoever, or for nothing at all, not even a possibility.

But still, how do I know all this? By making the experiment of thinking out consequences of the view, and consequences of its denial, in order to see in which case absurdities result. The absurdities may show themselves in various ways, but never as mere conflicts with fact. Thus the man who says he has no faith in God, but goes on living, thereby shows, one may argue, that he has faith in *something*. Let him explain what the something is. I believe that, unless it is God, it will turn out not to fit the faith he has in it. You may say that it is mere empirical fact that the man goes on living and thus exhibits, in Santayana's phrase, some sort of "animal faith." But suppose he does not go on living; he then ceases to take part in the argument or to have any opinion concerning God. So the indispensability of faith is a logical one, inherent in thinking as such. In any world whatever, living, and therefore thinking, in that world would express faith of some sort, and I believe the full intelligibility of the faith would always point to God and his essential attributes of power, goodness, and wisdom.

Once more, how do I know all this to be correct? If "knowledge" means having opinions tested by relevant tests then I claim to have some approach to knowledge in this matter. Making this claim does not *establish* it, but merely invites others to offer their counterclaims so that we can pursue the inquiry further. I have faith that I am on the right path. But there is no use merely declaiming this rightness. I can only try to make my faith intelligible to others.

So far, I have talked as though the term "God" had a fairly definite meaning, and the chief question was whether or not this meaning corresponded to reality. But there are competing conceptions of deity, and we have to choose not simply between theistic and nontheistic philosophies, but also among diverse forms of theism. What is to determine this latter decision?

If there must be an intuitive or experiential basis for the religious idea, it seems reasonable to suppose that it is in some actual religion or religions that this intuition comes most clearly into consciousness. So, competing formulations of theism may be tested by asking: do they express the content of religion in its higher manifestations? Whatever meaning is assigned to the term "God," it ought to designate the One who is worshipped. If it be asked, "What is worship?" a remarkably lucid definition is implicit in the first "great commandment" of the Old and New Testaments. God is whatever is the adequate object of unstinted or wholehearted devotion, whatever could be loved with all one's being. Since nothing is as loveable as love itself, the other and more explicit New Testament definition of God as sheer love seems to be deducible. By this criterion, Aristotle's definition of God must be immediately rejected, for his God loves no one unless himself, and mere self-love is not particularly loveable. Spinoza's conception also fails, for a similar reason, as does that of Plotinus.

To make worship definitive of the divine nature may seem to be, but is not, a mere argument from an empirical fact, the fact that some people worship, or as one says, have "religious experience." On the contrary, it is not the *fact* but the *idea* of worship from which we derive the definition. Perhaps no one, in fact, loves God, or anything else, with "all his being." Who could prove that he or another man does this? The point, however, is that we may be able to understand the *ideal* of such a complete devotion. God then is its appropriate recipient. To believe in him is to believe that if we do not worship, the fault is with us, not with the nonexistence of an appropriate recipient. Moreover, in any possible world in which there were sentient and thinking beings the question would be relevant: "Is there a suitable object of worship, of total devotion?"

To be the appropriate object of total devotion implies radically unique properties. Somehow all value, all meaning, everything even mildly interesting in any way, must be an aspect of God himself. For otherwise, there would be that much of our being which was concerned not with God but with something else. I am convinced that traditional theology failed adequately to understand this. If I see a man in need and try to help him, how can this interest in his need consist entirely in love for God, if God is defined—in the usual manner—as wholly self-sufficient, *ens a se,* wholly incapable of suffering, or of acquiring value from anything we do? Jesus said that in helping the needy we help him, and if this refers to Jesus *as God,* then God can be helped, and is not in every sense self-sufficient. Our interest in remedying evils must mean an interest in remedying something in God, not just in the world or in any man.

Suppose we take the other definition, that God himself is love. Again we have the question: "What does this mean, if God is simply self-sufficient, absolute, infinite, and incapable of being influenced by the world?" In my judgment, it means nothing at all, on the stated assumption. To love is to be related to, and influenced by, what is loved. Sympathy, participation, sorrowing with the sufferings of others and rejoicing with their joys, these are not dispensable aspects of love, or some inferior version of it; they are its essence. Without sympathy mere "doing good" to others is not love. The sun does good to us, but to all appearances loves us not. Divine love has been compared to the sun, or to a fountain, by those who wished to maintain the divine self-sufficiency. In this they have unwittingly exhibited their lack of interest in the lovingness of deity. A god who showers benefits upon all, but cares nothing for them, a "cosmic benefit machine," is what many philosophers and theologians offer us, not the God of the New Testament, or of any of the higher religions at their best. The only clear alternative to the benefit-machine idea is a God really related by sympathetic participation to his creatures.

We know well the chief historic source in the West of the identification of deity with self-sufficiency, rather than with love, properly so-called. This source is Greek philosophy. For Plato—at least as usually interpreted—and Aristotle, the divine may perhaps be loved but it does not love in return; and they held this view for the precise reason that love implies a certain qualification of self-sufficiency, a seeking and finding of part of one's own good in another than oneself. Medieval theologians wanted to have it both ways, without, so far as I can see, removing the contradiction. They wanted God to have all the self-sufficiency of the Greek deity, and yet so to love the world—and even (as Origen said) be moved by its misery—as to be motivated to send his only son to help mankind.

The more I read in the metaphysics of religion, the more I am impressed by the pervasive role of unnoticed ambiguity in confusing great minds. To say that God is self-sufficient, independent, absolute, the necessary being, has two possible meanings, not one. To see this, let us consider in what sense we creatures are lacking in self-sufficiency, independence, or necessity. That sense is that there is simply *no* quality of a man, however essential or inessential to his personality, which does not depend for its coming to be and its continuance upon antecedent or concomitant causes. Thus man, and the other creatures likewise, are in *every possible* respect dependent and contingent. This leaves open two ways of distinguishing God from his creatures: (1) We may suppose that, as the creatures are in *all* qualities dependent or contingent, so God is in all qualities independent or necessary. (2) We may suppose that God is in *some* qualities independent and necessary, but in other qualities dependent and contingent. The main mass of philosophers and theologians took the first way, while a tiny trickle, a most honorable trickle in my view, took the second. Those who took the first way seldom even saw the possibility of the second. This means that they answered a question they had never clearly asked. My philosophical methodology frowns upon such a procedure. If in philosophizing we choose one of two possible views, we should always know clearly what the other view is and why we reject it. The small minority which took the second way *of course* knew all about the first way; they could not help it, since the adherents of the first way dominated the seats of learning, and wrote nearly all the books. Thus only the partisans of the second view really knew what choice they were making, and insofar only they exhibited a sound methodology!

Since no mere creature is independent in any of its qualities, to exalt God above the creatures it suffices to ascribe to him independence in *some* appropriate quality. To go beyond this, and declare him independent in every quality is not justified by the legitimate requirement that there be a clear distinction between the worshipped and the worshippers, or between God and other realities. For only God can be self-sufficient in any quality whatever. By what right then do we follow Aristotle in making pure self-sufficiency equivalent to deity? Self-sufficiency in *some* respect is enough to establish an immeasurable gulf between God and other beings. Self-sufficiency in all respects is therefore at best superfluous for this purpose; but it is worse than superfluous, for it commits us, if we are intellectually serious, to the further Greek view that the gulf between us and God cannot be crossed by God, but only by us. Our love can perhaps reach up to God, but his "love" cannot reach down to us, for that must mean that we contribute some qualities to God, some joy arising from our joy, some sorrow arising from our suffering.

There is another ambiguity by which great men were confused. That we have qualities dependent upon others is not our real defect, which is, rather, that our dependence or limitation is itself a highly dependent or limited one. We depend greatly upon our neighbors, friends, or enemies, but scarcely at all upon multitudes of beings, say the inhabitants of another planet. And we shall *never* depend upon what remote posterity may do. Our dependence or limitation, then, is itself dependent or limited. What others can do to influence us depends upon what and where we and they are in the space-time world. Only an insignificant fraction of God's creatures can have an appreciable influence, and many can have no influence at all, upon us. Very different is the dependence of God upon his creatures. Since his love is the supreme and all-embracing love (otherwise he would not be a suitable object of total devotion) any creature whatever influences God, for its good gives him joy and its evil gives him sorrow. To deny God dependent qualities is then doubly superfluous in that, not only is his incomparable supremacy already guaranteed by his being self-sufficient in *some* of his qualities, but, in addition, there is a supreme way of having dependent qualities which is alone worthy of God, and possible only for him. This supreme way is the nondependent way of being dependent. The *scope* of God's dependency or conditioning is not subject to conditions, it is absolute. We depend upon some, he simply upon all.

The little word "all" is the real key to theistic metaphysics. God is, in certain of his qualities, independent of all things; in others he is dependent upon all. In the former aspect, God is first or supreme cause; in the latter, he is supreme consummation or effect. No creature is, in any respect, *either* cause of all *or* effect of all. Always the creature is cause of *some* things only, and effect of *some* things only. The creatures are individuals with nonuniversal functions, God the individual with universal functions. *Someness* is the creaturely trait, *allness* is divine. God loves and is loved by all; he is influenced by, and influences, all.

There is a symmetry in this view which I believe is a logical merit. It is, I incline to think, something like the sort of symmetry which has led physicists to accept certain views rather than others. The Greek-medieval view compares God with the creatures in a rather raggedly unsymmetrical fashion: thus, God causally influences *all,* we only *some* things; but God is influenced, *not*—as symmetry implies—by all but by none, while we are influenced, again, by some only. The sole ground for this lack of symmetry must be that to be influenced is felt to be in principle bad, a sign of inferiority. What basis is there for this prejudice? Our ethics does not embody it, no wisdom actually practiced expresses it. There is simply *nothing* wrong with being influenced, merely as such; though of course there are wrong ways of being influenced, just as there are wrong ways of influencing. The mother who rejoices over her son's virtue and happiness is surely not inferior to the one who is simply indifferent to a son's weal or woe. Rather the contrary. The thoughts of a zoologist are influenced by the amoeba or fruit fly he studies. This does not make him inferior to the amoeba or fly. I repeat, there is nothing wrong with being influenced.

The symmetrical view of the divine universality or all-relatedness is logically correlative to devotion as expressing all one's being. For when we take even the least interest in anything, this should, according to the ideal of worship, be an interest in God himself, and this is possible only if the divine life takes into itself all the forms of contingent reality, including even all sufferings. How then, you may ask, can there nevertheless be something absolute, self-sufficient, independent, or necessary in God's nature?

The answer lies in taking seriously the analogy between God and an individual person. This analogy, strangely enough, has, in the scholarly world, seldom been taken seriously. A person has a "character," a set of personality traits, which are relatively fixed in the midst of changing experiences and acts. If the acts are free, they are not wholly dictated by the character and circumstances, but are creative additions to the person's life. This distinction between the fixed or essential characteristics or personality traits, and inessential, changing details of experience and action, may be analogically, or in the "eminent" sense, applied to deity. God then has an invulnerable individuality or unique essence which makes him always "himself," no matter what additional qualities he may or may not acquire. The traditional "attributes," such as omniscience, properly interpreted, express this essential character of God. No matter what happens, God is eminently wise, good, and mighty; this attribute (for, as tradition rightly held, it is really but one) God possesses necessarily and self-sufficiently. We do not make God wise, good, or mighty, and we could not make him otherwise. We can, however, contribute to the empirical *content* which God wisely, righteously, and mightily receives from the world. We do not determine the infallibility with which God knows the content, the creation; we only determine something of what is infallibly known. Infallibility, by itself, is a mere abstraction; only the content can make it concrete. True, it is not in our power to decide whether or not God shall have concrete content, for his supreme creative power presumably guarantees that he will have some world or other. But we can determine something of the richness and beauty of the world God infallibly knows.

In a sense, the final meaning of God for the creatures is not in what he may do for them, but in what they may do for him. We are all, with all our qualities, contributions to his imperishable life, which alone can appreciate us in our full value. In this way it is literally true that the aim of all creation is the divine glory. Many seem to value God as means to their own future safety and comfort. But serving God now should be our comfort. This doctrine may be termed "contributionism." "Our lives, our souls and bodies," are thus "a reasonable and holy sacrifice" unto him.

Does this mean that God loves us only for himself? No, for it is only because he loves us for ourselves, in our unique actuality, that we contribute anything to his life. Love *is* essentially participation, appropriation of the life of the other into one's own life. To suppose that this is true only of inferior or creaturely forms of love, while God's love is sheer benevolence without appropriation, sympathy, or receptivity is to forget that our human capacity for taking into our own lives that of others is as severely limited, at least, as our benevolence. The ideal form of sympathy is possible only for God. To say that it is unworthy even of him is to make it a strictly homeless ideal. Infinite receptivity is no less superhuman than infinite independence. Both, I submit, belong to God, and to God alone. To adapt Whitehead's witty saying, men refused to give unto God what could not belong even unto Caesar.

Those who have read Tsanoff's *Crossroads of Religion* will probably have noticed some similarities between the view of deity therein set forth and the view which I have defended in this essay. Professor Tsanoff is one of a number of recent writers, well-informed concerning the "great tradition" in religious metaphysics, who have realized that this tradition is capable of improvement in more than trivial aspects and that when these improvements are made, the case for positivism or agnosticism loses at least part of its cogency. In the present century it is this country which has been richest in such writers, and Tsanoff is not the only one of them bequeathed to us by some foreign land. In Europe freedom from the past has, in our sad century, been realized chiefly through nihilistic rejection of metaphysics. In our more hopeful society it is possible to think both freshly and constructively.

SOVEREIGNTY AND THE IDEA OF REPUBLIC

by Charles W. Hendel

Preface.

Statesmanship is a noble and difficult art and it is rare. And to criticize or complain about the conduct of public affairs is of course easy. It is not becoming in a philosopher who has learned from Plato and Spinoza that "all noble things are as difficult as they are rare" to pretend rashly to know better than those charged with such heavy responsibilities of state and daily engaged in negotiations involving military, economic and political power as well as the imponderables of opinion and belief. It is also well to remember Machiavelli's observation: "Fortune is the arbiter of one half of our actions . . . she leaves us to direct the other half, or perhaps a little less."[1] Even *virtù supreme* may be defeated by circumstances. We should not in a superior, self-righteous manner lay any failure, then, simply to the faults of particular men or governments.

Yet in our present democratic world it is permissible, even the duty of any one in any nation whose life and prospects of well-being or ill are subject to the train of consequences that follow from acts of government and diplomacy to speak out when things seem wrong or bad. And in such a situation, it may well be the office of a citizen devoted to philosophy to examine the frame of ideas in terms of which the diplomatists and politicians speak to each other and to the world and formulate their hoped-for settlements. Sometimes the troubles do come from a poverty of ideas, or it may even be from a lack of coherence in them which prevents any consistent policy from being attainable and in such situations the services of philosophers can surely be of some use.

1. The Case that Raised the Question of this Paper: The Suez Canal Affair.

What is here to be presented as a subject for discussion is occasioned by the Suez Canal imbroglio of recent occurrence. Three civilized nations in the pursuance of their rights have employed force against Egypt and left a blemish on their great records. There was young Israel seeking to secure her very existence, itself so unwelcome and intolerable to her neighbors and they themselves will allow of no possibility of peace, and so a state of belligerency is thrust upon Israel willy-nilly and used as a ground for debarment from what had been an "international" waterway. Along with Israel, or at least acting at the same time, were France, so long a leader in civilization and culture, and Britain, the modern world's school for political-freedom under law, these two old states high in honor. They took their military action and entered the land of Egypt. Yet one fine day or so they all "folded up their tents and silently stole away."

What made the victors do this, retreating from the positions of vantage which they had gained? That may not be so easy to answer in a few superficial words. More than meets the eye is involved, along with the public reasons. Thus we may hear it said, for instance, that Russia had growled with an ominous threat. The United States of America openly showed disapproval, together with some resentment at not being consulted. The United Nations voiced the general demand that member nations must not cope with a unilateral abrogation of conventions in that aggressive fashion but ought to proceed through the proper agencies of peaceful solution. There was a suspicion, too, that the states interested in the Suez Company's claim had tried to effect a fait accompli that would alter the situation several years hence when the Canal was due to revert to Egypt. In such confusion of hidden purposes and announced policies, and seeing the obvious danger of a war in the Middle East which could bring on a total world war, the onlooker nations had somehow called a halt, and their words had been heeded.

2. The Question Concerns Sovereignty.

It is at this constructive juncture that the doubts and questionings arise concerning the quality of our contemporary statesmanship. The diplomats of the West seem always to be at the mercy of situations others have created. They improvise for each such occasion: now a user's association and virtual boycott, then payment under protest to obdurate Egypt. There is also a troubleshooter from the United States wandering amid the foreign offices of the Arab nations in hopes of making friends and influencing people. Here helpless drift is all one sees, and no real settlement in prospect. Nothing has resulted except bulletins of reassuring words of comfort that all will be well, but nothing is proposed that will bring the nations together under the rule of law. We are still waiting for a *policy,* one course of action with some kind of unified aim and showing the proximate, logical, practical steps toward the ultimate goal of an international order with the semblance of mutual security and freedom with justice. There is, however, one special troubling outcome of this whole affair, namely, that the "sovereignty" of Egypt over the Canal has been accepted and vindicated. Only this and nothing more, nothing about the paramount authority of the United Nations or of any law above the nations under whose rule they must conduct their affairs and dealings with each other. All the governments concerned have had to bow before the sacred character of the sovereignty of one nation. They have not challenged the idea or even said in reference to sovereignty what it means or entails. In granting that Egypt has sovereignty they have recognized mere possession as true property, without looking into the title. They have conferred a benefit for a previous violation of a convention and they have tied their hands so that they cannot put law above sovereignty, and all this is a very great evil.

3. *A Profession of Faith.*

I have passed a judgment here. Before going on to the properly philosophical part of this presentation let me confess the full content of my convictions. It is my belief that in thus bowing and scraping deferentially before sovereignty—I mean national sovereignty, and this applies to any nation whatsoever—the politicians and lawyers of the present age are condemning us to still further reversions from peace and a decent civilization. I have taken the Suez Canal case only as an illustration and may have misjudged and misrepresented it. Let it be treated as a fiction, then, or a myth. The point I want to bring out is that the featuring of the sovereignty of any state as untouchable and absolute so that one cannot argue about its competence or propose limitations is contrary to the philosophy of the "republic" which I hold to be the only foundation for civilized existence. The idea of "republic" includes a number of ideas with which the idea of sovereignty is in opposition. This contrariety among the ideas that are essential stock in the trade of politics can be one cause for the failures of the policies of great powers from which we are suffering. I believe that we must commit ourselves steadily to the republic-idea and do all that it requires of us or else perish. So much for the profession of faith.

4. *Concerning "Ideas."*

Every idea long acceptable and valuable in the experience of people is more than a single concept. It has first some original intent, and then it develops a set of essential meanings which are logically and empirically connected. When the term is used that refers to this schematic idea it may actually call up the thought of only a part of the system but more is entailed, and sooner or later it may come to light. One may recall here what Immanuel Kant said about the meaning of "idea" in Plato, and the idea of the "republic" as an example.[2] The actual employment of any "idea" from time to time in history results also in certain historical associations which become adherent to its meaning and these may be as influential and important and fateful as the original sense. One can say, therefore, of the idea of republic as well as that of sovereignty what Chief Justice Charles E. Hughes said of liberty in an opinion of the Supreme Court: "Liberty in each of its phases has a history and a connotation."[3]

5. The Vogue of the Title "Republic" and Its Connotation.

Nearly all the nations of the world today are committed, by their own profession, to the political system of a republic or commonwealth. They have assumed the title and glory in it. It is an interesting historical phenomenon that during the past two centuries republics have come into such vogue. Besides the first republics of North, Central and South America and France, new ones, both large and small, have been established in Europe, Asia, and Africa. The fact that there is a Republic of China and a Union of Soviet Socialist Republics shows that the idea has ubiquitous appeal across all ideological lines.

The connotation of "republic" in this present phase is largely determined by the American precedents. The colonists of British North America founded their republic, with help from France and Spain, and after a war for independence, from empire. They represented their cause as just before the rest of the world in immortal documents and claimed that the remote government in London had utterly disregarded the principles of free government, namely, the welfare of those governed and their rights and liberties. Liberated as a United States of America these people set up their own institutions, beginning with a constitution defining and limiting the powers of any subsequent government for the American nation. Meanwhile the French Revolution occurred, a throwing off by the people of the intolerable yoke of their own government. The Republics of Ibero America were a close sequel revealing to the world that the idea of republic was not limited in meaning and value to peoples of British and French extraction but was viable for nations of other stocks and traditions and cultures. And all these republics were established with difficulty and in the teeth of greater power elsewhere which might at any time conspire to wipe them off the face of the earth. With their hardy survival and dramatic success the name "republic" is historically associated.

So for many years, as nations have developed strength and integrity within former empire and revolted or freed themselves, they have assumed this proud title of republic. It signifies liberation from domination and an autonomy or self-government and dedication to the principle that the proper object of all government is the general good. Usually, too, conditions have been established defining and limiting powers of government in the interest of personal liberty. This is the connotation of republic in its recent phase.

6. The 18th Century American Version: the Republic with Personal Liberty.

The idea which has thus entered into modern civilization is of course ancient, and everyone naturally thinks of the delineation in the *Republic* of Plato. It is well to recall the speculative daring of philosophy in those days, and how the exemplar Socrates set out bravely to explore, in the face of ridicule, the sheer possibilities of the idea which ran far beyond any actual reality and even to sketch a whole order of society where the ideal might be completely realized. Though the scheme as a whole has seemed ever Utopian, parts of it have more than once been appropriated with remarkable effect. And an instance was the founding of the first American republic. The statesmen of that epoch worked from a pattern of republic which was mediated to them through Locke, Hume, and Montesquieu. Indeed, Montesquieu's *Spirit of the Laws* was a remarkably fertile reinterpretation of the Greek view of community and politics as applying to many types of historical situation vastly distant from anything contemplated by Plato and Aristotle. Inspired by such "republican" philosophy, the Americans then achieved their own original adaptation of the idea. "Republican government" to them meant not only adopting the central proposition of the Platonic politics, viz., that the general good shall always be the end of government, but also introducing the modern and "democratical" proposition that the people themselves must be represented in the government so as to be able to determine the laws and policies that in their opinion best serve the welfare of the nation. Thus provision for personal liberty was welded into the traditional form of the republic.

7. The Original Platonic Pattern in Review.

Immensely viable as this eighteenth century version has been, it should not be assumed to exhaust the possibilities of the republic-idea. The civilized world, organized in part, at least, according to such "republican principles," is now in dire straits and in need of a redeeming policy and we might profitably consult the original speculative pattern once again and try again, too, to put philosophy into good practice.

Let us consult, then, or better, review the scheme sketched by Plato. The first intention is to counter an evil pervading all parts of human society, viz., the Thrasymachus spirit and its sophistry: Power is not only its own law but it also imposes upon those subject to it, "the weaker," a belief that this is right. In actual fact such imposition can hardly succeed for long at a time simply because "justice" really is by "nature" something different from whatever merely prevails, and men even without philosophy do discover a real distinction between right and might.

That these are two things is matter of common experience, for life in society involves some reference both to justice and to force. There is then no reducing of one to the other. It is for the philosopher and the statesman instead to work out a rationale of both as realities that men must live by.

Power Harmonized with Justice: The First Intention of the Republic.

This harmonious order was not the peculiar dream of Socrates. It was writ large repeatedly in those various wonderful vehicles of Greek culture, the drama, the sculptured frieze, the reported counsels of the Delphic oracle, the celebrations of the Olympic games, as well as in histories and philosophies. It was sung early in the verse of Solon, the revered lawgiver of Athens who gloried in what he had done, in these words:

> "I liberated them. And through my power
> With force and justice in true harmony,
> I did the work."[4]

In the Greek spirit, then, the primary intention of the *Republic* written by Plato is to show that force must be harnessed with justice and never allowed to run rampant into injustice.

Law Supreme—Justice.

With law-giving in mind (the Solon gift), it must be said of course, that governments make laws, too, and they order thereby the affairs of the State, but these positive laws are something other than the supreme rule governing the exercise of power. This supreme law or justice is not something to be manipulated by rulers according to their arbitrary judgment or will and it is, indeed, by reference to Law in that eminent form that particular laws are judged to merit the name and authority of law.

Harmonizing Self-Interest and the Commonweal in some Identity.

A second stipulation appears in the consideration of the actual situation as respects the government of men, a situation which the Greeks faced no less realistically than Hobbes was to do at a later time, Hobbes who had learned so much from Thucydides. The aspect of the matter in view was this: it is always men who will do the governing and men will naturally act for their own interest and private advantage. This is as much a reality in human affairs as is the existence of force, previously recognized, and again the solution is not to reduce one distinct thing to another but to harmonize them. Self-interest must be reconciled with the interest of the whole community, in some kind of identity, and neither one swallowed up in the other. The striving of men for their own good is legitimate and necessary but, inasmuch as there are so many different men with such varying abilities and powers no one can really promote his own welfare without attention to, and even acting on behalf of the general welfare of the community in which he "operates," so to speak.

Government Stands Under Law and the Public Good.

It has developed in the inquiry that both a public end (the objective of common good or the commonwealth) and a rule (justice) stand over the power of government. They are criteria by which acts of governance are judged. There is a higher law and a good transcendent to the ambitions of rulers. Hence these are essentials of the connotation of republic—the supremacy of law for the State itself and the paramount concern for the commonwealth and all its members.

Education a Superior Function to Government.

The subordinating of political power goes even further—but this one can barely mention here. Education has higher place and dignity in the society of a republic than government. None of the above stipulations for the good life—indeed even for survival—can be met in any degree until "every man, woman and child" is somehow imbued with the spirit of membership, concerned for the whole community, and persuaded of the rule of law. In proportion as men think and feel themselves members of one body and "care more for the community and for one another" ("The Phoenician Story," *Republic,* 414, 415), the more disposed they will be to govern their conduct from within and the more responsibly will they behave toward each other. The lessons in self-government are hardest for the ones of political capacity, for such men "are guilty of the greatest crimes from ambition" (Aristotle, *Politics,* 267a), and it is they especially who most need an education in what Montesquieu flatly called "self-renunciation."[5]

The Connotation of Republic.

These are the minimum essentials of the systematic idea of republic as set forth by Plato, and relevant to the purposes of our discussion—they are not regarded, however, as exhaustive of its meaning: A republic is an order of society founded upon a sense of community and membership where men feel responsibility and are inwardly determined to exercise self-restraint out of regard for the whole State and for their fellows, and an order where a higher law than the laws of the State regulates all men and governments alike. Only in such a system can force and self-interest be combined with justice for all in the whole commonwealth and men go forward together into the natural competitions and enjoyments of a social existence without destroying one another and many possibilities of good in themselves and others. And the tenets of the republic are not a set of stipulations only for a pleasant and good living, they are the condition of survival.

8. *Sovereignty: The Original Phase.*

The Raison d'Etre.

Historically sovereignty is associated with the establishing of order out of the chaotic state of affairs in sixteenth and seventeenth century Europe characterized by religious schism and civil dissension within and wars between the various nations. Some authority was imperative, for the universal authority, be it Church or Empire, had become ineffectual to control the situation. The changing economy, too, demanded ever new law without delay and such law could not be that described by Aristotle which "derives all its strength from custom," and "requires long time to establish."[6] The answer to the imperative need was new practice and new theory in support of it, the theory of the sovereignty of the State.

An Addendum to the Republic.

In Jean Bodin's *Six Books of the Republic* the idea of sovereignty was introduced under the wing of that of republic: The supreme importance of the republic-idea was evident because in a time of such bitter, fanatical, disrupting religious warfare and the contests of princes with rival armies, all elements in society needed to be reminded of the idea of the State as one commonwealth whose preservation and welfare are paramount above all other interests and whose substance ought not to be wasted in internecine conflicts. The necessity of an authoritative rule of law was obvious. And the new design of authority was conceived to secure unity, order and law in each of the particular states, for henceforth there had to be many Sovereignties, corresponding to the territorial States.

The First Intention: Absolute Power to Make Law.

In Bodin's words, "sovereignty is the absolute and perpetual power of the republic to dispose of the goods and persons of the entire State . . ."[7] The primary feature of this absolute sovereignty is that it is a power-with-right to make laws without the consent of the governed.[8]

Power Absolute Yet with Limitations.

Absolute though it be called, sovereignty in this historical connotation was no glorification of power unlimited: Bodin, Grotius and others who developed this first meaning intended their own theories as counterblasts at the amoral teachings of Machiavelli (Bodin, *op cit.,* explicitly Chap. 9). They conceived all the universe as under natural law which, as the law of God, stood supreme over all powers and principalities whatsoever. The sovereign was absolute but under God, and absolute, therefore, only in the sense that no other earthly agency within or beyond the national State had any "right" to intervene and restrain this sovereign power. But sovereignty was also more particularly limited. It was itself a case of the property right under the law of nature, and were the exercise of it to weaken the validity of such natural-law property right it would actually sap its own foundation. It was further limited *de facto* by the "law of nations" insofar as it was to the interest of other powers to maintain that public law. Further still, and of dubious value, sovereignty was limited by the moral law that required "good faith" and the observance of agreements and contracts. But vis-à-vis private parties, families, corporate bodies, etc., within the State, sovereignty was absolute in that it had the right and authority to command action in accordance with the sovereign will.

The Original Connotation Compatible with the Idea of Republic.

As thus introduced, in a milieu of respect for natural and moral law, the idea of sovereignty was not yet contrary in any important sense to the ancient idea of republic and it was proper of Bodin to present it to the learned and political world as a version of the "republic" relevant to the times. But a contrariety was latent. Were the belief in natural law to weaken or fade into thin air, the law of the sovereign State would rule absolutely supreme and unrestrained. To be sure, limited sovereignty, limited by new "constitutional" law, might salve the republic idea and its values unless something happened further to exalt the power of the State so that it could readily override all moral compunction and the restraints of the law of the constitution.

9. Sovereignty: The Nationalistic Phase.

A sequence of developments must briefly be noted without time to argue for or justify them in this presentation.

From Monarchy to Sovereignty of the People.

In practice sovereignty in its first phase was associated almost exclusively with monarchy and centralized government. In due season monarchical power was overthrown. The gloriole of supremacy passed from monarchs to the people: the sovereign-people substituted for the sovereign-monarch. Was it the same power, or less or greater?

Sovereignty Unlimited.

Greater, we must say, and for several reasons or causes. The general conception of natural law itself as moral law sanctioned through religious belief passed into the discard—the political world thought and acted without reference to over-arching law. Moreover, sovereignty, when attached to the "people," gained a new, peculiar *moral* quality, being in a sense a transcendent virtue available through the moral union of the wills of men. Thus sovereignty, in the new shift of weight, could gain upon law. Such sovereignty of the people would seem to need no limitation: it might be quite self-controlled.

The Theory of Rousseau.

So it was in theory, the theory of Rousseau. For Rousseau built two governing criteria into his doctrine of sovereignty. The "general will" was truly so—and therefore properly designated sovereignty—because it was general in its *source* (the wills of people uniting themselves in spite of their diversity of interests) and general in its *object,* viz., the general good of the whole body, each one and all of the people. Sovereignty is real then only in acting according to law which obliges and benefits every last one of the people equally. If that be so, sovereignty is actually limited by a stipulation that it shall ever establish only "equal law." Thus law again is the criterion and the very mark by which it is determined whether or not a putative sovereign has true sovereignty. Some writers see in Rousseau's philosophy of politics only the absoluteness and infallibility of the sovereign people, who thus seem to inherit the exemption from higher judgment expressed in the old maxim: "The King can do no wrong." It should be noted, however, that the title of the relevant chapter in the *Social Contract* is in the form of a question: "Whether the general will can err?"

The intention of Rousseau is very clear and plain in his last political work:

> To put the Law really above man is a problem of politics which I compare to that of squaring the circle in geometry. Solve that problem, and the government founded on the solution will be good and without abuse. But until then, rest assured that when you think you are making the Laws rule, it is really men who will do the ruling.[9]

Here is the ancient vision of the republic together with the supremacy of law. But Rousseau's system has been taken only partially—and dangerously so—in the political views of the two centuries since he published, though it fared better in philosophy, thanks to Kant.

Political Authority is Greatly Required in Modern Society.

Modern life still requires, as was necessary in the sixteenth century, the extensive functioning of government in making positive laws to take care of the relations of men and their disparate and highly competitive interests in the industrial and commercial economy of our era. The continuing increase of the power of government is not simply to be deplored or railed against to any effect. Political power must be available to bring into working harmony the powerful interests made possible by tremendous energies released through the scientific knowledge, the technology and the arts of organization in contemporary society. Call it sovereignty or something else, there must be legitimate authority with the power to cope with many divergent powers and bring them into order. The effective rule of Law is absolutely necessary.

10. The Critical Question of our Time.

Here is the critical juncture, and a question. Is sovereignty sovereign for the sake of law? Or is it absolute, and is law only the dictate of the sovereign? The fate of the system called the "republic" depends on the answer.

The trend of history in the very society of nations that so nobly call themselves republics seems fatal to the very system whose name they take. Nationalism has swept sovereignty-absolute into the saddle. The "will of the people" could in the past be a tame, academic, harmless thing, a mere x in a formula, any people, anywhere. But nations have for two hundred years become aware of their place and their time, their own group history, their defeats, their victories, their oppressions, their liberations—and their absolute separateness from other peoples. The "people" is a suppositious, universal, homogeneous thing and one may imagine a world organized as a republic or a republic of republics, but when the "nation" is the thing, it means *this* nation over against other nations; it means jealous boundaries of interest, seeking national gain alone and not seeing and caring about the cost of ruining competitors, treating with other nations but abusing the profession of good faith only in order the easier to take advantage of them. The nations can do no wrong in their own eyes, and since they judge only by reference to themselves there is no public right or law. Such sovereignty is absolved from respect for any higher law. Politicians can rant without rebuke from their constituency whose will they pretend to represent. "Who can flout the will of the people?" They quickly tell the people, too, what that will is. Thus liberty as well as law declines, when men do not have a will of their own and do not exercise it and let it be known. This is the dark scene of our time, with sovereignty in its nationalistic phase.

Sovereignty has gained a new absoluteness and it has also developed a new sophistry with which to sustain itself. A new Socratic argument is necessary to expose the frauds, to re-present the connotation of republic as it pertains to our circumstances, and to redeem liberty, the very liberty under law which the American nations have been particularly proud of in the past. Besides argument there must be action, enlightened by the discussion and guided by a politics which employs terms and ideas that are consistent or coherent, thus sustaining a policy which may advance the cause of civilization among the nations.

11. The Contrariety between Sovereignty and the Idea of Republic.

For the present, the point of what has been said is this: that sovereignty which is really absolute in fact and by pretension is contrary to the political system of society which is denominated that of the republic.

Such unlimited and uncontrollable sovereignty breaks away from the essential connection with right, from the harmony of power with justice, and from the subordination of government to law. Sovereignty in this mode is divested of both legal and moral quality and becomes nothing but sheer strength or power. It cannot claim therefore to be a right and to be respected as such. Such political power acknowledges no responsibility and it does not belong in a world that believes itself civilized, according to the criteria of civilization which have been profitably employed ever since the Greeks. It is the very prevention of peace among nations, the peace for which men have yearned and have striven hard. They will have no peace until they settle scores with nationalistic sovereignty. Plainest of all is the handwriting on the wall, that sovereignty in its unruly nationalistic form is the supreme threat to human liberty, that liberty which has been the very condition of the knowledge, the science, the developed economic power which has produced possibilities of well-being for all people greater than the world has ever known. The key to the future of liberty, law, international order and peace, is what one thinks and says and believes about such sovereignty. It is recommended here that we resume thinking seriously about the system of things which is symbolized by the term of "republic" and begin putting our ideas in order and making possible a practical diplomacy and politics which holds forth some hope for men of all nations.

NOTES

1. *The Prince,* trans. by W. K. Marriott (London and New York, 1908), p. 203.
2. *Kritik der reinen Vernunft,* A 313-318, B 369-375.
3. The Case of Near versus Minnesota, 1931.
4. *The Greek Poets,* ed. by Moses Hadas, trans. by Martin Ostwald (New York, 1953), p. 167.
5. *Spirit of the Laws,* Book IV, Ch. V. *See* C. W. Hendel, "To Montesquieu: Acknowledgment and Appreciation," *Revue Internationale de Philosophie* (November, 1955), pp. 346-365.
6. *Politics,* 1269a, trans. by William Ellis (London, 1888).
7. *Six Books of the Republic,* Ch. 8.
8. J. N. Figgis has declared that this concept of positive law, law made and enforced by the sovereign State, is distinctive of modern theory and practice as contrasted with the medieval and classical. *See* "Political Thought in the Sixteenth Century," *Cambridge Modern History* (New York, and Cambridge, England, 1934), III, Ch. 12, 745 ff.
9. C. W. Hendel, *J. J. Rousseau: Moralist* (2 vols., London and New York, 1934), II, 315. Translation from Rousseau's "Considerations on the Government of Poland." Original text in C. E. Vaughan, *The Political Writings of Rousseau* (2 vols., London, 1915), II, 426-7.

ON THE UNITY OF THE PRAGMATIC MOVEMENT

by Charles Morris

William James stressed in his *Pragmatism* that "the one" and "the many" are not contradictory categories by showing how the universe may be one in some respects and many in others. This insight applies to the pragmatic movement as well. To claim that there is an underlying unity in the movement is not to deny that there are important differences between the major pragmatists, differences in their problems, their emphases, and even in some of their doctrines. The pragmatic movement, like the universe, is "one" in certain respects and "many" in other respects. The present essay aims to investigate the sense in which American pragmatism is a unitary philosophic movement.

This task requires some guiding conception of what constitutes a philosophy. Since the term "philosophy" is today explicated in many, and often opposing, ways, it is necessary to choose some conception of philosophy to serve as a reference point for the analysis. A quite traditional point of view will be chosen: a philosophy, as a conception of the cosmos and man's place in it, includes a cosmology, a theory of value (axiology), and the acceptance of a certain method for conducting inquiry (epistemology and logic). Such a conception of philosophy is only one possible conception among many. Its choice is not, however, capricious, since it reflects a position, made explicit by the Stoics, which has dominated much of the history of philosophy. It will be claimed that the pragmatic movement has a cosmology, axiology, and methodology, and that these are integrated into a distinctive philosophical orientation through an actional or behavioral theory of signs (semiotic). The stated conception of philosophy provides the framework for the following analysis. The problem of the unity (or disunity) of the pragmatic movement would, of course, take different forms if other conceptions of philosophy were chosen.

I

We must now ask what is the distinctive focus of attention of the American pragmatists. That the basic focus is upon human action is unmistakable: the pragmatists are centrally concerned with man as actor. They are not, however, concerned with human action in all its aspects. As philosophers they center their attention upon thinking man, and hence upon reflective or deliberative action. Their approach to thinking man has certain characteristic features.

There is a clear post-Darwinian evolutionary undertone, a sense for the living creature in its physical and social background. Evolutionary biology inevitably raised the question as to the nature of mind, thought, and intelligence when approached within the evolutionary framework—and pragmatism may in part be conceived as a sustained attempt to answer this question.

Secondly, the acceptance of the evolutionary framework went along with a rejection of the traditional mind-body dualism. The pragmatists were from the beginning anti-Cartesian, and constitute one phase of what Arthur Lovejoy called the "revolt against dualism." The tendency to think of mentality as a form of action increasingly dominated their thinking. Finally, there is in all the pragmatists a great respect for scientific method, and the belief that philosophy was to align itself as far as possible with the scientific enterprise; even if the task of philosophy was not to be identified with that of science, it was not to be conceived in opposition to science.

The pragmatists' account of reflective human action was at the level of ordinary observation and was not based on experiment, but it was empirical in intent and direction. It is for this reason that the pragmatic orientation helped prepare the way for later developments in the behavioral sciences.

II

So oriented, the inquiry into thinking man led directly to the central place of the topic of meaning within the movement. Charles Peirce wished that philosophy become observational and cumulative like science, and so in effect proposed that philosophers use language as the scientist does. The oft-quoted statement of Peirce must bear quotation again: For "the typical experimentalist, you will find that whatever assertion you may make to him, he will either understand as meaning that if a given prescription for an experiment can be and ever is carried out in act, an experience of a given description will result, or else he will see no sense at all in what you say." This is to affirm that to an experimental scientist a sign signifies that *if one acts in a certain kind of way a certain kind of experience will result.*

The emphasis here is on the intrinsic relation of action and experience, an emphasis which brings together the actional and the empirical orientations of the pragmatists. Now this formulation is not the full story of Peirce's account of signs (or "meanings"), but it does form what might be called the "hard core" of the pragmatic position. It is accepted, with some differences of emphasis, by all the major pragmatists; and even where there are doubts as to the sufficiency of the "hard core" formulation, all the pragmatists accept the view that signs function within, and must be interpreted with respect to, action. This actional theory of signs (or "meanings"), this *behavioral semiotic,* is the central unifying principle of the pragmatic movement, and one of its most original contributions. This does not mean that such a behavioral semiotic was the historical starting point of the major pragmatists, nor that their interest in the relation of signs ("meanings") to action was everywhere the same, nor indeed that a sufficiently comprehensive behavioral semiotic was ever formulated by any of the main builders of the pragmatic movement.

Peirce expressed the conviction that the main features of his (and James') thought would have been substantially the same if the pragmatic maxim of meaning had never been formulated. His main logical and cosmological ideas preceded his papers on pragmatism. Pragmatism was for him essentially a formulation of the criterion for admissible hypotheses if one works within an essentially scientific mode of thought. His general analysis and classification of signs was originally explicated with reference to his metaphysical categories of Firstness, Secondness, and Thirdness, and it was never brought into a clear relation to his later formulation of pragmatism. It was not even "behavioral" in its original form; only in a late paper, unpublished in his lifetime, did he explicitly defend the position that in the final analysis the interpretant of a sign (the effect on the interpreter in virtue of which something is a sign) was a habit or disposition to respond. He never reworked his semiotic from this point of view; he never gave a detailed exposition of this late point of view with respect to many kinds of signs (such as mathematical and normative terms); he never raised the question as to how far his earlier metaphysical categories and doctrines were compatible with his late behavioral analysis of the interpretant of a sign.

Peirce, therefore, cannot be said to have presented a systematic and comprehensive behavioral semiotic. But his analysis in the pragmatic maxim of an inseparable relation of action and experience (in signs with a "rational purport"), and his view that the interpretants of such signs are habits or dispositions to action, clearly are foundation stones of a behavioral semiotic. Even his belief that there is a level of meaning in addition to that formulated in the pragmatic maxim (such as in the meaning of certain religious terms) still connects such meaning with action: the meaning of such terms is stated to lie in their contribution to rational self-controlled conduct. Even here meaning is explicated with reference to action. In this sense Peirce can be said to have moved toward a consistently behavioral conception of signs.

The situation is much the same with William James, but because of James' special moral and religious problems, there are some differences of emphasis. James in a sense begins where Peirce ends, by giving a slightly different interpretation of Peirce's pragmatic maxim. In this maxim, as we have seen, Peirce stressed the necessary relation of action and experience in the meaning of signs with "rational purport." James' own formulation of Peirce's pragmatic maxim is in terms of "what sensations we are to expect . . . , and what reactions we must prepare." Here there is not an essential relation but merely a conjunction of "sensations" and "reactions," and in some formulations the relation is even weaker: "or" takes the place of "and." In this looser formulation James can admit as meaningful doctrines which affect the action of their interpreters even if these doctrines do not predict specific perceptual experiences—and he gives certain metaphysical and religious doctrines as examples. Peirce had come to essentially the same result, but only by admitting a level of meaning over and above that formulated in the "hard core" pragmatic maxim; James reaches this position by a looser formulation of the pragmatic maxim itself. In both Peirce and James the meaning of signs is consistently viewed in the context of human action.

George H. Mead did not refer to Peirce or to James in the presentation of his analysis of meaning. His orientation, however, is distinctly and unqualifiedly behavioral. Of all the pragmatists, Mead is most seriously concerned with developing a general theory of human action. His particular contribution to a behavioral semiotic is his stress upon the basically social character of both nonlinguistic signs and the linguistic signs which are built upon them as a foundation. Human action is for him in origin social action. The first human signs arise when the beginning of a response of one person is reacted to by another person as an indication of later stages in the response of the first person. Mead called these "nonsignificant symbols"; they became "significant symbols" (or language symbols) when vocally produced sounds, operating in this context, carried the same indication to the person making the sound that it did to others who heard the sound and interpreted it by the tendencies to action which it provoked. The interpretant of a sign is thus for Mead—as for the later Peirce—a disposition to action occasioned by the sign. Mead, however, spelled out in detail, in a way that Peirce did not, the social context in which language originated and operated.

John Dewey takes over much of Mead's analysis. He extends the approach by a more explicit treatment of signs in art, and the normative signs that occur in evaluations. C. I. Lewis (whose orientation is to Peirce rather than to Mead) is especially concerned with the meaning of judgments of value and judgments of obligation. Some further reference to value terms will be made in later pages. Here it is sufficient to note that the later pragmatists, whether influenced more by Peirce or by Mead, extend, but continue to build upon, the behavioral analysis of meaning characteristic of the pragmatic movement from its beginning.

III

The stress upon the behavioral functioning of signs is closely related to the guiding interest of the pragmatists in reflecting or inquiring man. This underlines a second unifying theme of the pragmatic movement: *a behavioral theory of inquiry*. Inquiry, as the attempt at the reflective solution of a problem, is carried on by means of signs (signs of course do not function only in inquiry). Inquiry is itself seen as a form of action, a phase of action to solve problems within a wider course of action in which it is embedded. As a form of action, inquiry can of course encounter problems within its own development, and so there arises inquiry to deal with problems which arise in inquiry. To this extent inquiry can become autonomous (to use Dewey's term), as it does to a large degree in mathematics and theoretical science. But in the main, inquiry is for the sake of first-level problems encountered in the action of the living creature in its physical and social environment. Inquiry is ultimately for the sake of such actions. Inquiry into inquiry is only a special form of inquiry, and hence of action.

Such an account of inquiry seems to me to present views common to Peirce, Mead, and Dewey. The importance for the pragmatic movement of such a behavioral theory of inquiry can be made evident by the following considerations.

In the first place, on this account, the occurrence of inquiry presupposes the existence of behaving organisms and an environing world which in various ways supports and hinders their activities. It therefore presupposes a level of behavior antecedent to reflective or inquiring behavior, in which inquiry arises and to which it ministers. Similarly, inquiry into inquiry itself presupposes the occurrence of a body of inquiries which constitutes its own subject matter.

Next, it is evident that this behavioral stress upon inquiry has close connections with the pragmatist approach to the topic of truth. It is natural to look at truth in terms of inquiry, as, for instance, a property of signs which in a process of reflection resolve the problem which was their occasion, and hence permit the ongoing of the behavior in which they arose. If signs with "intellectual purport" signify, in the narrower Peircean formulation, that such and such would be observed consequent upon such and such action, then signs whose predictions are fulfilled might well be called "true"—either in the case of a particular inquiry or more generally in the case of a prolonged and continuing inquiry which extends over many (and perhaps an endless number of) specific problems of a common sort. This, of course, is not intended as a full account of the pragmatists' treatment of truth (for there are many differences in the various analyses) but to suggest that a common denominator is found in locating the problem of truth within the context of a behavioral theory of inquiry. If signs are behavioral at the core, then the "correspondence" of signs to "reality" must be restated in terms of the relation of signs to the total process of behavior-in-an-environment in which they occur.

In the third place, while Peirce admitted a number of forms of inquiry, he held that the scientific form of inquiry is superior to the others in that it is cooperative in nature and inherently self-corrective. While it would not follow from this that the solution of all problems must be sought through the scientific mode of inquiry, or even that all problems can be solved through such inquiry, all of the pragmatists do share Peirce's esteem for scientific inquiry and advocate its extension to a range of human problems.

In terms of these considerations it becomes evident that the direction of the pragmatic analysis has been to replace the traditional epistemology, in whole or in part, by the theory of inquiry. Epistemology in its Western postmedieval form was connected with a mind-body dualism, experience was regarded as mental and private, and the task of the theory of knowledge was to show how the thinking individual could come to know the material world and other minds—or why he could not do this. The pragmatist has held that the individual never finds himself in this predicament—that problems always arise within an area of the unproblematic, and that accordingly "the existence of the world" can never become a problem for knowledge. The theory of knowledge, to repeat, is replaced (in whole or in part) by a behavioral theory of inquiry. Such a development is one of the novel themes of the pragmatic movement.

It may be noted in passing that a similar shift occurs in the interpretation of logic. In a wide sense logic is regarded as part of the theory of signs (Peirce). The formal principles of logic are regarded by Dewey and Lewis as derived from successful inquiry and held as norms for the further prosecution of inquiry: Lewis speaks of them as "pragmatically a priori" and Dewey as "operationally a priori," both using these terms with respect to the conduct of inquiry.

IV

It is not easy to name satisfactorily the third characteristic theme of the pragmatic movement: it is *the approach to axiology (to values and evaluations) in terms of preferential behavior.* None of the pragmatists did in fact employ the term "preferential behavior." But it may serve as a general term covering what Dewey referred to as "selective-rejective behavior," what James had called "demands," and what R. B. Perry (taking off from James) spoke of as "interests." Preferential behavior, roughly characterized, is action which tends to favor or disfavor one object (thing, situation, idea, behavior) rather than another. It is positive preferential behavior if the object is favored; negative preferential behavior if the object is disfavored. A preferential-behavior axiology attempts to locate all values and evaluations within the context of preferential behavior. It seems to me that in this sense the axiology of pragmatism is a preferential-behavior axiology, even though this label was not applied by the thinkers here under consideration.

There are of course various ways in which the term "value" can be explicated with respect to preferential behavior. It might be suggested that a positive value is any object of positive preferential behavior. James seems to do this in holding that the essence of value is to satisfy a demand, as Perry later explicitly did in giving as the generic meaning of "value" "any object of any interest." I think this position is found in C. I. Lewis who finds the meaning of "immediate value" in the liking or preferring of some contents of immediate experience (other things having value only in the dispositional sense of their capacity to lead to such immediate value experiences). Dewey's position would limit the term "value" to those objects of positive preferential behavior which continue to be favored after a consideration of the consequences of favoring them. In spite of these differences in the range of denotation of the term, all these pragmatists appear to interpret value with respect to what we have here called preferential behavior.

Evaluations on this approach may be regarded as eventuations of those inquiries where the problem concerns what is to be favored as an object of preferential behavior. If all inquiry occurs within an area of the unproblematic, then value inquiries (in the distinctive normative sense) may be regarded as inquiries concerning values which occur within an area of unproblematic values, and which can be completed only with respect to such unproblematic values. Inquiries as to what objects and experiences are in fact preferred, or inquiries as to the capacity of objects to arouse or sustain preferences, are not normative value inquiries in this distinctive sense, for the resolution of the inquiry involves no judgments made on the basis of unproblematic values. C. I. Lewis' "judgments of value" (or judgments of good) seem in this sense to be nonnormative, while his "judgments of obligation" (or judgments of ought) seem to be distinctively normative.

There are important differences of emphasis in the axiology of the various pragmatists. Nevertheless, the distinctive mark of pragmatic axiology seems to lie in the approach to the topics of value and evaluations within the context of preferential behavior. When so approached, it seems to me that terms referring to values remain meaningful within the pragmatic theory of meaning, and that evaluations fall within the general pragmatic theory of inquiry. One can, if one wishes, limit "scientific inquiry" to nonnormative inquiry, and in this case distinctively normative inquiries are not scientific; but this decision should not obscure the fact that the main difference between scientific and normative inquiries lies in the fact that in (distinctively) normative inquiries it is preferential behavior that has become problematic and that the resolution of such value problems is always done with respect to unproblematic values. Since careful normative inquiry will need to take account of the results of nonnormative inquiries, no limit can be set to the potential importance of science in the furthering and improving of man's value decisions.

V

A fourth unifying doctrine in the pragmatic movement may be called *the semiosical conception of mind.* "Semiosis" is the term used by Peirce for a sign process; semiotic is then the study of semiosis. To hold that mental processes can be regarded as sign processes can then be called the semiosical conception of mind. On this view mind is not regarded as a substance, nor is mentality regarded as the intrinsic nature of any property or event—thus experience as such is not regarded as mental. Experience is mental only to the extent that signs are operating within it, that is, to the extent that behavior is sign-behavior. Neither the sign itself (the sign-vehicle), nor the sign's interpretant (as a disposition to respond in a certain way caused by the sign), nor the object signified is as such intrinsically mental; it is the semiosical process as a whole that is called mental. To say that an organism has a mind is to say that signs are operating in its behavior.

Peirce had maintained that mind is a sign developing according to the laws of inference. James had written that consciousness as a stuff did not exist, but only processes in which one aspect of experience functioned as substitute or sign for other portions of experience. Mead did not equate mentality with all sign processes, but only with signs which he called "significant symbols"—signs which had the same signification to their producers and their interpreters, a view which restricted mentality to organisms that engaged in language behavior. There are obvious differences in these various views, but their common core is in linking mind and mentality with the occurrence of sign processes.

VI

There remains the problem of the pragmatist cosmology. The term "cosmology" seems preferable in this connection to the term "metaphysics." The latter term was indeed used by Peirce, James, Dewey, and Lewis. However, Dewey later withdrew the term as applicable to his views, Mead tended to use the term as a term of disparagement, and Lewis meant by the term an analysis of basic categories and not a concern for cosmology. So the term "metaphysics" is hardly an appropriate term for what is here under consideration.

Regardless of terminology, pragmatism has a place for cosmology conceived as an empirically based study of generic characteristics of the cosmos. For the pragmatists, as we have seen, the "world that is there," "the experienced world," is not regarded as a whole as mental, subjective, or private—these latter terms being used to describe only certain features of the world that is there. Accordingly, there is no general problem of the "existence of the world": since for the pragmatists problems arise only within a context which is unproblematic, there is no context within which the "world that is there" could as a whole become a problem. It is then, from this point of view, legitimate to attempt to characterize certain general features of the world, provided that this can be done in terms whose application can be controlled by observation of this world. In this sense there can be a pragmatist cosmology, which would differ in generality from the particular and partial accounts of the world furnished by the special sciences.

It is, however, difficult to find a phrase which clearly signifies a conception of the cosmos common to all pragmatists. Here indeed the differences between the pragmatists loom very large: Peirce's "objective idealism," James' "world of pure experience," Dewey's "cultural naturalism" are cases in point. And if we say that the pragmatic cosmology is "evolutionary" or "temporalistic" or "activistic," then it can be replied that these are not traits distinctive of the pragmatist cosmology since they have been emphasized by other cosmologists as well. It might seem, accordingly, that in the cosmological area the thesis of the unity of the pragmatic movement breaks down.

I do not believe, however, that this is the case. For if human reflective behavior is as the pragmatist maintains it to be, then such behavior is itself part of the cosmos, and the rest of the cosmos must be such as to permit the occurrence of such behavior. Since such behavior occurs in the world that is there, it is legitimate to attempt to describe certain general characteristics of that world, and to note what features of the cosmos are required to make such behavior possible.

Peirce held that the most general characters of the cosmos were expressed in the three categories Firstness, Secondness, and Thirdness—which correspond in part to the notions of possibility, existence, and law (or habit). These were seen as pervasive cosmological traits; while all were "real," possibilities and laws did not "exist" in Peirce's sense of existence, since existence for Peirce involved dynamic interactions which were only possible between particular things. Peirce supported his doctrine of the categories by phenomenological observation, by appeal to the results of the special sciences, and by the analysis of certain features of sign processes (which as themselves real could be used as the basis for hypothetical generalizations about the cosmos as a whole). In regard to the latter point, Peirce argued that analysis disclosed three, and only three, forms of propositions, and these served to express the three characteristics of Firstness, Secondness, and Thirdness.

While other pragmatists do not use Peirce's terminology nor his particular method of analysis, I think it can be argued that the cosmological views of all the pragmatists find a place for possibilities, existences, and laws (or habits). Insofar as this could be maintained, it could be held that a fifth unifying doctrine of the pragmatic movement is *the cosmological doctrine of the reality of possibility, existence, and law (or habit).*

Rather than support this position by reference to the various pragmatists I will show that the reality of possibilities, existences, and laws (or habits) is revealed in the analysis of reflective intelligence upon which all the pragmatists focus their attention. Since other philosophers might well hold the cosmological doctrine in question, this particular approach will link the pragmatic version of this doctrine with the pragmatic views of action and reflection.

If action occurs within a world which facilitates or blocks the course of action, this is a clear case of Peirce's Secondness. If reflective behavior or inquiry serves to advance blocked action by a consideration of alternatives for the continuation of such action, then we have an instance of Peirce's Firstness—an instance of the reality of possibilities. And if signs essential to the conduct of inquiry involve dispositions to action as their interpretants, this is a case of Peirce's Thirdness—the reality of laws or habits. Since all the pragmatists hold a similar view of human reflection and an actional theory of signs, they could accept this analysis as support for the cosmology under consideration.

It may of course be asked about the justification of applying to the cosmos at large traits revealed in an analysis of human reflective action. The only answer open to the pragmatists would be to admit (as did Peirce) that this is indeed a hypothesis, subject to control by further inquiry.

This cosmological model is based upon a consideration of what is involved in human reflective action. If this basis is to be generalized, then terms such as "action in a world" must be generalized so that human action becomes only one form of action. Mead attempts to do this in his generalized usage of such terms as "perspective," "system," "sociality," and "emergence." In his cosmology human reflective intelligence becomes one complex emergent level of processes which in a generalized form appear in nonhuman organisms and in the inorganic world. There are problems as to how far Mead succeeds in this ambitious attempt, the detailed elaboration of which was prevented by his unexpected death. Whatever may be thought of Mead's success, it is of great theoretical interest to attempt to construct a cosmological theory on a biosocial basis, in contrast to the basis in physics which has been the starting point of most modern cosmological models.

One point may be added. Peirce called his cosmology an "objective idealism," while Dewey's (and Mead's) cosmology is a form of "naturalism." The ground for this difference is worth noting. Peirce's idealism is supported by his interpretation of all forms of Thirdness as essentially semiosical. Since he applied the term "mind" to all sign processes, mind became a general cosmological category; and since he thought cosmic evolution moved by Thirdness converting Firstness into determinate forms of Secondness, mind became for him the dominant form of reality. But for Mead (and for Dewey) "mind" is restricted to certain high-level sign processes, and has no such dominant cosmological position that it had in Peirce. Hence an "idealistic" cosmology is supplanted by a "naturalistic" one. The issues here depend on the interpretation of the doctrine of continuity. Peirce at times calls continuity a methodological doctrine, but in general he converts it into a cosmological doctrine. Mead's acceptance of emergence permits discontinuities to be as basic (as "real") as continuities, and certain symbolic processes (and hence mind) are attributed to man alone, even though these sign processes emerge in evolution from animal sign processes of a simpler, nonlinguistic sort. Hence for Mead no cosmological idealism results.

VII

Such in outline is the argument of this essay that the pragmatic movement has an underlying unity. It reveals a number of common themes in its doctrines of epistemology as the theory of inquiry, axiology as the study of preferential behavior, and cosmology as the doctrine of the reality of Firstness, Secondness, and Thirdness. The doctrine of the semiosical nature of mind may be included within cosmology. It was further argued that all of these doctrines were linked with a behavioral semiotic, elaborated in the context of inquiry into the nature of human reflection. Except in one instance, attention has not been paid to the differences among pragmatists, nor the reasons for these differences. But this would be another study.

PLATO'S GODS

by Glenn R. Morrow

> Beloved Pan, and all ye other gods who haunt this place, give me beauty in the inner man, and may my outward person be at peace with the self within. May I consider him to be wealthy who is wise, and as for gold, let me have only so much as a temperate man can bear and carry. Anything more, Phaedrus? The prayer, I think, is enough. Let us go.

This prayer of Socrates at the end of the *Phaedrus* makes an intriguing close to one of Plato's most enigmatic dialogues. It is something of a shock to the modern reader to hear Socrates address such an earnest petition to the god Pan. This strange deity of Arcadia, half goat and half man, hardly qualifies in our eyes as a divinity at all. With his shaggy crooked legs and saucy tail, his cloven hooves and the amorous leer on his goatish face, he seems more comical than divine, especially when he is playing on his pipes and cavorting with the naiads and nymphs of the woods. If he is really a god, his appearance belies it; he is actually a striking illustration of that disharmony between the outer and the inner man which Socrates prays to be delivered from. And to the cultivated Athenian also Pan must have appeared as something of an oaf. Though his cult was popular among shepherds and farmers, it counted for little at Athens, maintaining only a precarious foothold in a grotto on the steep north slope of the Acropolis, well below the temples of the great gods Athena and Poseidon and the hero Erechtheus above. And who are the "other gods" associated with Pan in Socrates' petition? Certainly not the great gods of the Olympian family—not Zeus, nor Athena, nor Apollo—but local divinities of a minor sort, the water naiads and woodland nymphs with whom Pan loves to dally, and who have been mentioned incidentally in the opening pages of the dialogue.

From the artistic point of view this concluding episode is, of course, superbly appropriate. Socrates and Phaedrus have begun their séance with a discussion of the nature of Love. Socrates has shown that it is a form of madness, the kind of mental state that Pan was thought to produce on occasion; our own word "panic" carries the trace of this ancient bit of folklore. Socrates has gone on to show that Love is a divine madness, not an affliction, however, but one of the greatest of heaven's blessings, for it is the passion that underlies the soul's desire for eternity and for the vision of truth. And this divine madness seems to take possession of Socrates as he continues; he is admittedly under an influence outside himself as he describes the soul's effort to follow its god up the steep ascent of heaven and obtain a glimpse of the superheavenly realm. This "inspired" myth, as Socrates himself describes it, is followed abruptly by a descent to the solid ground of rhetoric and dialectic, and Socrates engages in a long discussion of the technical requirements of artistic discourse and of the procedures of analysis and synthesis which are indispensable to the philosopher. This prosaic sequel is so prolonged that we are in danger of forgetting our starting point, and thus it is appropriate that after it is concluded we should be reminded again of the divine source of that madness which both afflicts and blesses the philosopher. And the setting of the dialogue fairly dictates the choice of the god whom Socrates should invoke for this purpose. The talk has taken place in the country, just outside the walls of Athens, on a warm summer day. Socrates and Phaedrus have been lying on the soft green grass, under the shade of a big plane tree, dangling their feet in the cool waters of the Ilissus, listening to the song of the cicadas, and feeling the soft summer breeze on their faces. In short, they have exposed themselves with abandon to the magic influences of nature at the season when we are most susceptible to them. Indeed it is the inspiration of this "holy place," as Socrates calls it, that moves him to give utterance to his splendid myth about the soul and her aspirations. What other god could Socrates invoke at the end than this god Pan, the personification of all these gracious influences of nature?

There is a second element of dramatic fitness in this closing episode, when we recall the Socrates whom Plato has portrayed in the *Apology* and the *Phaedo*. A man of scrupulous piety, he always has at his side an unseen companion, his daimonion, who has often restrained him, and has done so in this very dialogue, when he was about to do something impious. This is the Socrates who, as Plato portrays him, regarded his whole public career at Athens as a divinely appointed mission to his fellow citizens, a mission enjoined by the oracle at Delphi; the Socrates who took his dreams so seriously that he spent a part of his last days in prison composing an ode to Apollo, lest he inadvertently disobey a divine injunction that he should "make music," and whose last words were a reminder to Crito to sacrifice a cock to Asclepius. The Socrates here is thus fully in character when he appears as so sensitive to the requirements of piety that he does not overlook his obligations even to the minor deities of the Greek pantheon.

But this suggests a further and more difficult question. Is this episode appropriate to the character of Plato? We cannot doubt that Plato's was a profoundly religious mind; but it was also creative, in religion as in other areas, and we know that he had a philosophical conception of God which went far beyond the ideas of his countrymen, a conception of one God, the source of all goodness and order in the world. This is in fact so close to the Judaeo-Christian conception that it gave powerful support to the Hellenistic Jews and to the early Christian thinkers in their efforts to construct a philosophical theology. For us, now that they have done their work, the great god Pan is dead. Could he really have been very much alive, we ask, in the mind of the man whose thought helped later generations to do away with him? Dead also are the high gods of Olympus, in all their splendor, with their trains of daemons and lesser divinities whom Plato has just described in Socrates' great myth. How could Plato—or Socrates, either, for that matter—have believed seriously in their existence and their effects on men and nature? Surely, we say, they must have seen through these make-believe divinities and recognized the folly of worshipping them. Indeed, does not Plato tell us as much in those passages where he criticizes Homer and Hesiod for their tales about the gods? If these passages are to be taken seriously, then this one in the *Phaedrus,* and the many others in the dialogues which seem to be expressions of honest piety, can only be concessions to the conventions of his countrymen.

Ordinarily it appears like a breach of propriety to inquire closely into a man's religious beliefs; they are too intimate and personal, and a man is entitled to his privacy. If he uses the language of piety which is current among his fellowmen, we are ready to accept it as a necessary means of communicating his sentiments to them, and we readily pardon him the slight insincerity involved if their language is not precisely his. But Plato was not an ordinary man. His figure is such a towering one, and his character has been so diversely appraised by his admirers and his detractors, that an inquiry into his private attitude toward these gods of his countrymen seems justified. For if there is insincerity here, how can we fail to suspect a lack of candor about the other matters on which he professes to instruct us? But if we wish to find out what Plato's sentiments really were, where shall we look for them?

The dialogue form in which Plato casts all his writings often serves as a mask to obscure the author behind the words and thoughts of his characters. But in some of the dialogues the mask is more transparent than in others; and of them all, the *Laws* seems to offer the best opportunity to determine Plato's own thoughts on this particular question. Socrates does not appear in the *Laws,* so that the "Socratic problem" does not plague us here. His place is taken by an Athenian Stranger whose interests and experiences are so similar to Plato's, as we know them from other ancient testimony, that we cannot avoid taking him as a thin disguise for Plato himself. For one thing, this Athenian Stranger is represented as advising a Cretan friend, with the aid of a second companion, a Spartan, concerning the constitution and laws for a new city that is to be founded in Crete. This is the sort of undertaking that the members of the Academy under Plato's leadership were frequently engaged in, as we learn from other ancient sources, and Plato's aid in some such enterprise had been invoked on at least three well-attested occasions. Plato had acquired a certain prestige as head of these highbrow legislators in the Academy and a reputation for competence in such matters; and this is the position ascribed to the Athenian Stranger in the *Laws*. Furthermore, the dialogue mask itself is much less prominent and sometimes is taken off altogether. During long stretches of the work, including parts that are highly relevant to our present question, we have simply a straightforward exposition by the Athenian, his companions listening like students at a professor's lecture. Here, then, if anywhere, it seems that we can catch the words of the real Plato. The religious institutions that he prescribes for this imaginary city ought to furnish unambiguous evidence of his own attitude toward the religion of his time, particularly since the city to be established is a new foundation, without history or traditions, and offering carte blanche to the legislator.

If then Plato had thought that the old Greek religion was dead,[1] here was a chance for him to propose a new form of worship for his colonists at the beginning of their political life. Religions, of course, cannot be invented by philosophers, and Plato certainly knew this; but a disapproving philosopher would hardly have copied so slavishly as Plato does the religion of his people. For it is the familiar Greek religion that he proposes for this new state, with its pantheon of Zeus and the other twelve gods and their host of attendant deities, and with the familiar sacrifices, dances, games, and festivals connected with their time-honored worship. This system of observances is never presented together as a systematic whole, but what is more telling, is inserted item by item at relevant points of the legislation, sometimes merely by a bare reference which invites the reader to supply details that the author does not think it necessary to spell out in full. Each area of conduct, each chapter of the code of laws, is under the special patronage of a familiar god. Zeus, for example, is the protector of the oath (the Zeus Horkios of Greek liturgy), the protector of the stranger and suppliant (again familiar roles; those of Zeus Xenios and Zeus Hikesios); he is also the protector of boundaries (Zeus Horios), and with Hermes is the guardian of heralds and ambassadors. Athena is the patroness of the arts and crafts; she is especially offended, for instance, if the artisan does not receive his pay. Apollo is the patron of dance and song, and through them of the whole system of education. Hera supervises marriage and the rights of women;

the fines levied for breach of the marriage laws are deposited in her temple. Dionysus is the giver of wine, of Bacchic dances and ecstatic revelry, and the patron of Plato's quaint institution of the "chorus of elders" whose function it is to set the higher standard of singing and dancing. These elderly gentlemen will clearly need the stimulus of wine to carry out their duties properly. There is even a familiar but nameless deity, the goddess of the highways (*enodia daimon*), who looks after objects that travellers have left behind them. The gods of the underworld, dread Hades and his assistants, appear in Plato's legislation, for it is to them that funeral sacrifices and ceremonies are performed. Bloodshed in all its forms, accidental, passionate, or deliberate, must be purged in accordance with the time-honored procedures laid down by the oracle at Delphi. Even the Eleusinian mysteries, an important and honored part of Athenian worship, appear in Plato's state, though of course without their Athenian designation, for this is to be a Cretan colony. Not merely is the whole of Plato's legislation sprinkled with such pious details, but the traditional religion even underlies the political structure of the state. Each of the twelve tribes has one of the twelve gods as its special patron; each subdivision of the tribe is to be under the patronage of one or other of the gods, daemons, or heroes; and every household is to have its hearthside worship to its family gods. Elections of officers take place in sacred areas adjacent to the temples of the gods we have mentioned; jurors in the courts swear by Zeus and Hestia to render an honest verdict; and judges in the court for capital offences "pass through slain victims" (a phrase from religious law) as they deposit their votes on the altar of Hestia. And so on.

All these details are presented with such scrupulous adherence to the niceties of Greek ritual and observance that it is obvious the author knows his religious law thoroughly and respects it. In fact it is laid down as a guiding principle that the legislator must refrain from altering in the slightest degree the sacrifices and rites that are already established in the area of the new colony. Plato regards all these traditional practices as having the authority of the oracles, those holy places where God declares his will to men. Of these oracles three were especially sacred in classical times, those of Dodona, of Ammon, and of Delphi; all three had played an important part throughout the archaic and the classical periods in regulating religious worship, for example in establishing new cults and modifying old ones, in transferring the bones of heroes, in adjusting the boundaries of sacred areas and protecting them from encroachment. Plato mentions all these oracles, but in his time the oracle of Apollo enjoyed the most widespread authority and prestige. Apollo's sanctuary at Delphi had become, in a real sense, the religious center of the Greek world, an oracle whose advice was sought, when possible, on every important occasion in the life of an individual or a city, and whose instructions could be flouted only with the greatest circumspection. So will it be in Plato's model city. "We must bring from Delphi laws about all matters of religion," says the Athenian Stranger (759c).

This massive body of evidence, of which I have only scratched the surface, shows how punctiliously Plato adopts the religious practices of his time in all their details. But this result is undeniably puzzling. It suggests that the philosophical legislator in Plato has completely abdicated his function in the area of religion, and we find it hard to believe that Plato really intends to do this, unless we can see a philosophical reason for it. And when we remember the passages referred to earlier in which Plato criticizes Homer and the other poets for the unedifying and immoral tales they tell about the gods, our puzzlement increases. How can Plato be reconciled with himself when he reinstates these gods for worship in his model city?

A variety of divergent explanations has been given for this seeming inconsistency. The *Laws* is a work of Plato's old age, certainly written after his sixtieth year; and it has often been suggested that it only shows that Plato, like many lesser men, became more susceptible, as he grew older, to the religious teachings he had learned in childhood. In his youth he had been a philosopher and critic; in his old age sentiment and tradition took over, obscuring the philosopher in him. This explanation, though plausible in general, will not do for our particular difficulty, for the decision to defer to Delphi in all matters of religion is not the decision of the aged Plato. The remark of the Athenian Stranger just quoted merely reaffirms a principle that Plato had laid down many years before in the *Republic,* in a passage that is often overlooked. After Socrates has completed his first sketch of the ideal state, Glaucon asks what part of the legislation still remains to be laid down.

> "For us nothing," Socrates replies, "but for the Apollo of Delphi the chief, the fairest, and the first of enactments."
>
> "And what are these?" asks Glaucon.
>
> "Sacrifices, and the founding of temples, and other services of worship to gods, daemons, and heroes. . . . For we who are founding the city know nothing of such matters, nor if we are wise shall we use any other interpreter than our ancestral one. For this God who delivers his interpretation from his seat in the middle and at the very navel of the earth is surely the ancestral interpreter in religious matters for all mankind" (427bc).

No religious institutions are in fact prescribed in the *Republic,* and this passage tells us why. It is not because they are unimportant—on the contrary they are "the chief, the fairest, and the first of enactments"—but because they lie outside the competence of the secular legislator. Thus it is not a reversal of Plato's former position but rather a reaffirmation of it when the Athenian Stranger in the *Laws* says that we must go to Delphi for laws on all matters of religion.

Another common explanation is that Plato simply recognizes the futility of trying to eradicate these firmly rooted beliefs and practices of his countrymen; and since his purpose is to draw the outlines of a practicable program for the Greece of his day, he has no alternative but to acquiesce in them. The authority of a legislator is limited; and even the founder of a new colony, though its members are to be drawn from different parts of Greece, could not hope to do away with the religious traditions that all his colonists will have in common. Thus it is said that Plato admits, though reluctantly, these traditional beliefs and practices. The difficulty with this explanation is that if it were true, we should expect Plato to leave these unnecessary and uncongenial practices alone, trusting that in the course of time they would wither away of their own weakness. We should not expect to find him strengthening them by providing for a more meticulous enforcement of religious requirements, and formulating—as he does—a drastic law against impiety, a law which, so far as we know, had its historical parallel in few Greek cities, perhaps only at Athens. It looks rather as if Plato thought that the Greeks of his day were beginning to neglect their religion, and that to correct this degeneration in the religious life of his time the state must protect it—and not only protect it, but control it, so far as that is consistent with the authority of Delphi.

Finally there is a more cynical interpretation. It has been said that Plato, himself indifferent to the appeal of these old gods, is proceeding in the spirit of a thoroughly realistic, if not cynical, legislator who sees the utility of religious sanctions for insuring obedience to law, and adopts, as the handiest and most useful means for accomplishing his legislative purpose, the practices that have the strength of long Greek tradition behind them. Plato's own cousin Critias had been a realist of this sort. In a fragment of one of his poems we find him explaining the belief in gods as the invention of some ancient "wise and crafty statesman" seeking a means of deterring men from secret wrongdoing.[2] The memory of Critias was not held in honor by later Athenians, but this legal-utilitarian theory of the origin and function of religion may have been widely shared by his contemporaries, emancipated as they had been by the teaching of the Sophists. We find echoes of it in Euripides, and it was certainly not forgotten by fourth-century statesmen. Plato too was well aware of this law-supporting function of religion, and himself frequently invokes the sanctions of divine displeasure and punishment in a future life to deter transgressors. To be effective, such divine sanctions must be presented in vivid concrete terms; and what would be better adapted to this purpose than the familiar apparatus of Zeus with his thunderbolts and the underworld gods with their pitchforks and scourges?

But upon reflection it becomes clear that the explanation offered does not cover all the facts; it explains only a part, and that the less important part, of the role of religion in Plato's state. The function of religion is analogous to the function of law which it supports. Plato declares that the purpose of law is not so much to punish transgressors as to educate all the citizens; likewise he regards the policing function of religion as subordinate to its positive role in molding the citizens' character. Before attempting further to solve the puzzle with which we have been dealing, let us see how Plato conceives of this positive function of religion, and then we may properly ask how he could have thought that the religion of his countrymen could discharge it.

The nature and function of religious worship are set forth in solemn words by the Athenian Stranger at the beginning of the prologue to his legislation in Book IV:

> God who, as the ancient tradition tells us, holds the beginning, the end, and the middle of all that is, moves through the cycle of nature straight to his goal. In his train follows Dike, the punisher of those who fall short of the divine law; and she in turn is followed, in humility and orderliness, by every mortal who would be happy; while he who is lifted up with pride, whether of wealth or power or youthful beauty, and has a soul hot with insolence and thinks that he needs no guide or ruler but is able himself to be the guide of others, he, I say, is left deserted of God (716a).

The language of this solemn passage is clearly an echo of the great myth in the *Phaedrus,* which pictures Zeus at the head of the procession of the gods, all of them with their trains of worshippers, climbing the steep ascent of heaven, some of the followers managing to keep in their lord's train, others falling out and being left behind.

> What line of conduct, then, the Athenian Stranger continues, is dear to God and a following of him? One only, that which is expressed in the ancient proverb that "like is dear to like" . . . . Therefore he who would be dear to God must, so far as is possible, be like him and such as he is. Consequently the temperate man among us is the friend of God, for he is like him; whereas the intemperate and the unjust are unlike and at variance with him (716cd).

The imitation of God is a theme that runs like a golden thread through Plato's later dialogues. Recall the eloquent passage of the *Theaetetus* in which Socrates declares that the ultimate bliss of the philosopher is to become like God, through withdrawal from the petty details of this world to the heights of contemplation (175b-177a). What we have just read from the *Laws* is the same doctrine, transposed from the philosophical to the religious key. Philosophy is the exercise of thought, the practice of dialectic; but religion is the practice of worship, and worship is rooted in the feelings. The essence of worship is the sentiment of reverence, Plato believes, reverence for forms of being higher than ourselves; and the practice of worship is the performance of acts of devotion and dedication to these higher beings. Through worship a man recalls them to his mind and reenforces his sentiments of reverence; in worship he is actually assimilated, for a time at least, to the god whom he worships. To be effective, such worship must be habitual, reminding the citizen at frequent intervals of these higher forms of being, recalling those sentiments that are likely to be crowded out of mind by the cares of ordinary life, and confirming by repeated dedication the worshipper's commitment to his god. Religious worship, as thus conceived, is for Plato one of the most important factors in molding the character and training the sentiments by which a man becomes really just, temperate, and courageous. This is the specific way in which religion supports and supplements law, viz., by developing an emotional attachment, an enduring and quasi-instinctive love, for those virtues which good citizenship requires. This area of tradition and reverence is what Plato regards as the divine sanctions to the performance of our duties. There is another kind of sanction, that of prudential reason; reason shows us, if we reflect upon the various kinds of pleasure and pain and the kinds of life they accompany, that the choice of temperance, courage, and wisdom is the most conducive to happiness. The practice of worship, then, is in full accord with the judgment of practical reason; but religion has a more immediate and an immensely greater effectiveness because it acts directly upon the sentiments, and thus prepares a man for the ready acceptance of what reason pronounces to be best (732e-734e).

Religious worship, then, is not an exchange of services between men and gods, as might be supposed from an unthinking inspection of religious ritual, and as is in fact suggested by Euthyphro in his dialogue with Socrates. Rather it is this ritual, adorned with dance, song, and prayer, by which the nature of the gods is brought vividly before the worshipper for admiration and imitation. The favor that it procures is not an external reward for the correct performance of the rites, but the fellowship of the gods and their approbation of the worshipper's character. And the consequences of it will be the "divine goods," i.e., the virtues in which man's true happiness consists. Therefore, the Athenian Stranger concludes,

> For a good man to engage continually in sacrifice and communion with the gods, by prayers and dedications and all kinds of worship, is an exceedingly good and glorious thing and most conducive to a happy life (716d).

But can the Greek gods furnish the patterns for imitation which this conception of worship requires? Surely not the gods as sometimes pictured by the poets and mythmakers. Not the Zeus who mutilated his father Kronos; not the Apollo who seduced Creusa and concealed his escapade; not the Ares and Aphrodite engaged in secret amours, nor the Hera who quarrels with Zeus, nor the Zeus who tries to keep his infidelities from her. These lustful, bickering, jealous gods, susceptible to bribes and flattery, partial to their favorites among mortals and vengeful towards those who have aroused their displeasure—these are not the models of orderliness and virtue which we should want our citizens to admire and imitate. Socrates declares roundly in the *Republic* that such tales about the gods are not to be permitted in the state. The *Laws* shows that Plato was of the same mind in later life and gives us additional examples of improper tales. Hermes was not a thief, no matter what the poets say (941b); the story of Zeus's infatuation for Ganymede is a fiction of the Cretans to justify their own lawless passions (636c); and as for the legend that Hera made Dionysus mad and that his gift of wine and Bacchic dancing was an act of vengeance, this is an affront to both divinities (672b). All this shows that Plato, although he sets up the Greek gods as objects of worship, repudiates a large part of the mythology that had gathered about them.

Since the mythology is all that most of us know about these gods, it seems at first sight inconsistent to accept the gods and reject their mythology. But to suppose that there is inconsistency here is to misunderstand Greek religion. Mythology was not worship; the myths were a poetic embroidery on the cults, the product of that impetuous Greek fancy that could not refrain from giving to every numinous figure a concrete appearance, a local habitation, and a history. The very variety of these myths and their mutual incompatibility show that they did not constitute a systematic theology, or a set of beliefs which it was impious to question or deny. The poet was apparently free to reject or modify an earlier myth according to his own or his hearers' pleasure. No, the heart of Greek religion was not in mythology, but in worship, in the observance of the practices of the cult, as they had been established by long tradition and regulated by the oracle at Delphi.[3] Such worship implied, of course, an acknowledgement of the deities to whom sacrifices, prayers, and dedications were offered, and an acknowledgement of their authority over the lives of men, each in its traditional area of conduct and prescription. But there is no evidence that Greek religious law required any but the most general beliefs about the nature and history of these divine sponsors of the moral law. Plato's own law against impiety is equally general in its requirements. What Plato's law demands is only belief that the gods exist, that they have a care for men, and that they cannot be turned aside from justice by special offerings and ceremonies. There will be poets in Plato's state (even in the *Republic* this is implied [607a]) whose function it will be to embroider these bare elements of belief with poetry and song and myth, as Plato has embroidered his own philosophical doctrines, and they will presumably be free to add imaginative elements as they please, provided only that they present true pictures of these divine beings.

Bearing this in mind, let us take another look at the passage in the *Republic* in which Plato criticizes the poets. Through all the Christian ages it has been tempting to think that he is writing here like some Saint Augustine born before his time, advocating a purified monotheism in opposition to the degenerate polytheism of his people. But to read it so is to ignore the clear words of the text and to miss the important point that Socrates is making. He is not saying merely that the poets, in telling the tales mentioned, are false to the nature of the true God; it is in the name of the traditional gods themselves that he brands their accounts as lies. He is saying that Zeus, if truly represented, could not be pictured as deceiving mortals to their undoing (*Rep.* 383a) or as overcome by anger (378d) or lust (390b); he rejects these and other such tales, not because they are portrayals of make-believe gods, but because they are false tales of recognized gods, the gods of the Greek pantheon. It is true that Socrates in this same passage also speaks of God, in the singular, and asserts that these tales are false representations of His nature. This is one of the many passages in which Plato uses "God" and "gods" in the same context, with no indication of a distinction in meaning between the two terms. And so we sometimes ask, "Was Plato really a monotheist or a polytheist?" The answer seems to be that he was both, as even a modern Christian often is—for example, when he dedicates a cathedral to St. John the Divine, or builds a shrine to the Virgin, or prays to St. Anthony. In any case, what arouses Plato's indignation is that these tales are travesties of the gods of Greek worship, the gods whom the citizens in his state are to honor and reverence.

Furthermore, this passage does not say that such tales are all that one will find in Homer and the poets about the gods. Indeed, to find examples of what Plato would probably regard as true representations of the gods we need look no further than to Homer himself. Think, for example, of the last book of the *Iliad,* where the grief-stricken Priam, bearing offerings, goes to the tent of Achilles to ask for the body of Hector. Zeus himself in his pity has planned this solution to a problem too difficult for the human actors to resolve, and has himself inspired these two pitiful mortals to play the parts assigned them—Priam to risk his life and sacrifice his dignity by visiting the Greek camp and appearing as a suppliant before the slayer of his son, Achilles to forget his wrath and accept Priam's offering as an honorable price for the body of his hated enemy. As Priam and his herald, with the wagon bearing the precious gifts, leave the city walls and descend into the plain, Zeus sees them and sends Hermes to give them safe guidance. Recall how Hermes, in human guise, meets them casually at nightfall as they reach the stockade surrounding the camp of the Achaeans; how he leads them safely in the darkness, the while consoling the old man with praise of the dead Hector and with assurances that the body is still fresh and undecayed; how he lingers about Achilles' tent during the conference between the two tragic actors and later during Priam's restful sleep in the porch when the ransom has been effected; and how he wakes him before dawn and hustles him away before the enemy warriors are up and about. This surely is an authentic picture of divine providence, of divine companionship and consolation.

Similar pictures of the gods are to be found elsewhere in Homer, and in all stages of Greek poetry. The sculptors' work paralleled that of the poets. The modern student can still see, for example in the surviving marbles of the temple of Zeus at Olympia, how the sculptors caught the lineaments of the divine in their images of stone. We can see the majesty of Apollo in the west pediment, quelling the brawl between the Lapiths and the Centaurs; and in the fragments of the twelve metopes that once formed a frieze over the temple doors we can see the tenderness, grace and power of Athena as she attends Heracles during the performance of the twelve celebrated labors. One of these metopes pictures Heracles carrying the burden of the earth while Atlas goes to collect the apples of the Hesperides for him; here Athena assists the straining Heracles by a light pressure from below with the palm of her left hand—an unforgettable portrayal of effortless power. Nor can anyone who has seen it easily forget the figure of the mourning Athena in the National Museum at Athens, as she leans on her spear and gazes sadly at a tablet containing names of Athenian warriors who have lost their lives in their city's defence. There can be no doubt that these images, whether in words or in stone, spoke to the Greek worshipper even more movingly than they do to us. The great statue of Zeus which Phidias created for the temple at Olympia has disappeared and we can no longer read with our own eyes the message it carried, but we can read what Dion Chrysostom said of it: "Whoever among mankind is wholly weary in soul, whoever has experienced many sorrows and misfortunes in life, he, I think, if he stood before this statue would forget all the calamities and griefs that come in the life of man" (*Orat. XII,* 209M, 400R).

These and other similar portrayals of the gods in Greek literature make it easier for us to understand that Plato could regard the religion of his people as providing genuine objects of reverence and therefore as capable of discharging the important function of religious worship in his state.

Just because there was no official or orthodox mythology, these images of the gods were still plastic, and could take on new splendor and become even more adequate representations of the divine, as the developing culture and moral insight of their worshippers demanded. Pindar and Aeschylus had found this religion a vehicle for the expression of their profoundest insights and aspirations, while modifying this vehicle to accord with these deeper insights. Plato's was a mind of similar mold. This being so, I cannot doubt that the language of piety found in the dialogues is Plato's native language, as natural an expression for his religious sentiments as the Attic Greek in which these sentiments are phrased.

But did Plato, as a philosopher, really believe in the existence of the Olympian gods? The question must be asked here at the end, though it is very difficult, indeed impossible to answer without clarifying the terms of our question in ways which Plato's writings suggest but which they do not explicitly authorize. An object of worship is one thing, an object of scientific or philosophical thought is something quite different. It is clear, I think, that Plato did not regard the Olympians as objects of scientific knowledge. The *Timaeus* is quite explicit on that point. The *Timaeus* is indeed profoundly theistic; it pictures the generation of the cosmos as the work of a cosmic Demiurge, an artificer-god who frames the world and all its parts to the best of his ability; this hypothesis Plato boldly proposes as the most plausible explanation of the beauty and order of the cosmos. But the traditional gods of the Greek cosmogonies he accepts only with a certain irony. "Those who have given us these accounts were, as they say, descendants of the gods, and surely they must have known who their ancestors were. We cannot doubt the word of the children of the gods" (40d). This delightfully illogical defense surely indicates scepticism, especially since these traditions are said to be without the support of any necessary or even probable reasoning. Even more telling is Socrates' forthright statement in the *Phaedrus*: "We have never seen nor adequately conceived God, but we imagine him as a kind of immortal creature possessing both a soul and a body combined in a unity which is to last forever" (246c). These gods with immortal bodies as well as immortal souls, these are obviously the traditional Olympian deities, the gods of the poets, the painters and the sculptors, and these are said to be products of imagination, not scientific thought. Finally there is a significant *ignoratio elenchi* in the theological argument in the tenth book of the *Laws*. The Athenian Stranger advances this argument as a means of persuading the sceptics that they are wrong in denying the existence of the gods established by law (885b); but what the argument establishes is not the existence of the Olympians, but the reality of the philosophers' god, the cosmic Nous, or the "best soul," which we must assume as the explanation of the structure and orderly motions of the cosmos.

Yet unless this argument in the *Laws* is completely irrelevant to its context and to the persuasion that it purports to effect, there must be some relation between this God established by philosophical argument and the divinities whose worship is prescribed in Plato's state. There is something lacking in Plato's argument which the reader is expected to supply. I suggest that the missing link is Plato's favorite metaphor of the paradigm and its copies. Just as the worshipper imitates his god, so these gods whom he worships are themselves imitations, or images, of the divine principle revealed to philosophical intelligence; they are sensuous personifications of that wise and providential influence that manifests itself in all the course of nature and human life, but whose essence can be grasped only by philosophical thought. As imitations of that high God, they participate in the authority enjoyed by their archetype, and are worthy of worship according to the fidelity with which they represent His nature to our imagination. But they are objects of worship, not forces in nature, least of all forces which we can bend to our purposes; and there is no form of wrongdoing mentioned in Plato's legislation which he regards as more reprehensible than the practice of magic, or the pretence of it (909ab, 933a-c). It is significant that he regards this as the gravest form of impiety. It is more than a denial of the gods' existence; it rests upon a complete distortion of what their existence means for a genuine worshipper. Thus Plato remains a philosopher, but at the same time recognizes and makes a place for the legitimate and necessary demands of religious worship.

We are told that Plato erected in the Academy a shrine to Apollo and the Muses. If he participated in public worship with his countrymen, of which we can have no doubt, it would be in prayers and sacrifices to the gods of his people. As a philosopher he could only regard these gods as pictorial representations of the divine being whose nature can be truly apprehended only by nonsensuous thought; but as a poet and mythmaker himself, one of the most accomplished mythmakers of all times, he could take genuine delight in contemplating these godlike members of the Greek pantheon and through them worship the God of whom they were imitations.

NOTES

1. Wilamowitz comes close to saying this. *Glaube der Hellenen* (Berlin, 1931-2), II, 244.
2. Cf. Diels, *Fragmente der Vorsokratiker*[6] (Berlin, 1922), II, 387.
3. *See* Bruno Snell, *The Discovery of the Mind* (Oxford, 1953), 25ff., 128.

ABOUT THE AUTHORS

VIRGIL C. ALDRICH: Before joining the Department of Philosophy at the University of North Carolina in 1965, Professor Aldrich taught philosophy at Rice, Columbia, Brown, the University of Michigan, and Kenyon College. He also directed the Kyoto American Studies Seminar in Japan. He has served as President of the American Philosophical Association, Western Division, and Chairman of the Publications Committee of that organization. He was awarded the L.H.D. degree by Ohio Wesleyan. He has published widely in philosophical journals and is the author of *Philosophy of Art.*

VAN METER AMES: Having gone through the University of Chicago's educational steps from the first grade to the Ph.D. in 1924, Professor Ames joined the Department of Philosophy of the University of Cincinnati in 1925. He is presently head of the department and Obed J. Wilson Professor of Ethics, and is also Fellow of the Graduate School. He has served as visiting professor at Cornell, the University of Texas, and the University of Hawaii. Following a Rockefeller grant in 1948 to study contemporary French philosophy, he taught at Aix-Marseille in 1949. He taught at Komazawa (a Soto Zen university in Tokyo) while on a Fulbright research grant in 1958-59. He served as President of the Western Division of the American Philosophical Association in 1959-60, and President of the American Society for Aesthetics in 1961-62. He has contributed to philosophical journals and is the author of *Aesthetics of the Novel; Introduction to Beauty; Out of Iowa* (a poem); *Proust and Santayana; André Gide; Japan and Zen* (with Betty B. Ames); *Zen and American Thought;* and editor of *Beyond Theology: The Autobiography of Edward Scribner Ames.*

CLIFFORD BARRETT: Before taking on the duties of Chairman of the Department of Philosophy at Scripps College and Claremont Graduate School, Professor Barrett taught at Princeton and at the University of California in Los Angeles. He also held appointments at the College of William and Mary, and at Harvard, and served as Honors Examiner at Swarthmore College. He edited and contributed to *Contemporary Idealism in America,* and is the author of *Ethics; Philosophy;* and *Government of Law;* and of a forthcoming book, *Norms of a Rule of Law.*

CORNELIUS A. BENJAMIN: Professor Benjamin received his undergraduate and graduate education at the University of Michigan, and also studied at the Sorbonne and Cambridge University. Before joining the University of Missouri, where he was Chairman of the Department of Philosophy for many years, Professor Benjamin taught at the University of Chicago. He is a past President of the American Philosophical Association, Western Division. He has held a Guggenheim Fellowship, and is a Fellow of the American Association of Arts and Sciences. Besides numerous contributions to scholarly journals, his publications include: *Logical Structure of Science; Introduction to the Philosophy of Science; Operationism;* and, most recently, *Science, Technology, and Human Values.*

GEORGE BOAS: Awarded the B.A. and the M.A. in English from Brown University, Professor Boas' advanced degrees are in philosophy, the M.A. from Harvard, and the Ph.D. (1917) from the University of California. He holds honorary degrees from five other universities and colleges. He is a member of the American Philosophical Association, the American Academy of Arts and Sciences, and an honorary member of the Académie Royale de Belgique. Emeritus Professor of Philosophy at Johns Hopkins University, he continues to teach in universities across the nation. His books include: *Wingless Pegasus; Dominant Themes of Modern Philosophy; The Inquiring Mind; The Limits of Reason; The Challenge of Science; What Is a Picture?* (with Harold H. Wrenn); and *The Heaven of Invention.*

CAMPBELL A. GARNETT: Born in Australia, Professor Garnett has taught at the University of Adelaide, at Butler University in Indianapolis, and, from 1937-65, at the University of Wisconsin, where he served as Chairman of the Department of Philosophy. He is now teaching at Texas Christian University. In 1960-61 he was President of the Western Division of the American Philosophical Association. The most recent of his numerous publications are: *The Moral Nature of Man; Religion and the Moral Life; Ethics: A Critical Introduction;* and *The Perceptual Process.*

CHARLES HARTSHORNE: After receiving the A.B. (1921), M.A. (1922), and the Ph.D. from Harvard (1923), Charles Hartshorne studied in Germany at the universities of Freiburg and Marburg. He has taught at Chicago, and at Emory, and held visiting appointments at Stanford University, New School for Social Research, the University of Melbourne, the University of Washington, and Kyoto University. He is presently Ashbel Smith Professor of Philosophy at the University of Texas. He has served as President of the Western Division of the American Philosophical Association, and of the Southern Society for Philosophy and Psychology. He is co-editor, with Paul Weiss, of the first six volumes of *The Collected Papers of Charles S. Peirce,* and is the author of *The Philosophy and Psychology of Sensation; The Divine Relativity* (Terry Lectures, Yale);

The Logic of Perfection (which was awarded the Lecomte du Noüy prize); *Anselm's Discovery;* and of many other books and articles.

CHARLES WILLIAM HENDEL: Awarded the B.Litt. (1913) and the Ph.D. (1917) by Princeton University, Professor Hendel has also studied at Marburg University and the College de France. He has taught at Princeton, and at McGill, where he served as Chairman of the Philosophy Department and Dean of the Faculty of Arts and Sciences. Presently Sheldon Clarke Professor of Moral Philosophy and Metaphysics Emeritus at Yale University, he served formerly as Chairman of the Department of Philosophy of that university. In 1962-63 he delivered the Gifford Lectures in Natural Theology at the University of Glasgow, Scotland. He has served as President of the American Philosophical Association, and of the American Society for Political and Legal Philosophy. His publications include: *Studies in the Philosophy of David Hume* (two editions); *Jean-Jacques Rousseau: Moralist; Civilization and Religion* (Rockwell Lectures at Rice); *Freedom and Authority; The Philosophy of Kant and Our Modern World;* and *John Dewey and the Experimental Spirit in Philosophy.*

CHARLES MORRIS: Beginning his teaching career in philosophy at The Rice Institute in 1925, Charles Morris went to the University of Chicago in 1931, and since 1958 has been Research Professor in Philosophy at the University of Florida. He is a Fellow of the American Academy of Arts and Sciences, and the author of *Signs, Language, and Behavior; Paths of Life; Varieties of Human Value;* and *Signification and Significance.* Professor Morris did his graduate work in philosophy at the University of Chicago during the last years of the "Chicago School" of pragmatism, and is now writing a book on the pragmatic movement in philosophy.

GLENN R. MORROW: Professor Morrow received the A.B. from Westminster College (1914), and the Ph.D. from Cornell University (1921). He has taught at Cornell University, the University of Missouri, the University of Illinois, and the University of Pennsylvania. He was an American Field Service Fellow in Paris, a Guggenheim Fellow in Athens, and a Fulbright Scholar in Oxford. He served as President of the Western Division of the American Philosophical Association in 1939, and of the Eastern Division of the same organization in 1953. Besides many articles in journals, Professor Morrow is the author of the following books: *The Ethical and Economic Theories of Adam Smith; Studies in the Platonic Epistles* (two editions); *Plato's Law of Slavery;* and *Plato's Cretan City.*

JAMES STREET FULTON: Holding the B.A. and the M.A. from Vanderbilt University, and the Ph.D. from Cornell (1934), Professor Fulton taught at McGill University, at Shrivenham, and at Yale University before coming to The Rice Institute in 1946. He has been Chairman of the Department of Philosophy at Rice since 1956, and has also served since 1957 as Master of Will Rice College, and, during 1964, as Acting Dean of Humanities. He is the author of *Science and Man's Hope,* and articles in scholarly journals.

KONSTANTIN KOLENDA: Professor Kolenda received the B.A. from The Rice Institute in 1950, where he was introduced to philosophy by R. A. Tsanoff. For three years he was Susan Linn Sage Fellow in Philosophy at Cornell University, and received the Ph.D. degree from that university in 1953. That year he joined the staff at Rice, where he is now Professor of Philosophy. As a Fulbright Scholar he lectured on American philosophy at the University of Heidelberg in 1959-60. In addition to articles in scholarly journals, his publications include a translation of Arthur Schopenhauer's *Essay on the Freedom of the Will,* and a book entitled *The Freedom of Reason.*

SELECTED BIBLIOGRAPHY OF THE WRITINGS OF RADOSLAV A. TSANOFF

This bibliography does not include articles, stories, and verse published in Bulgarian journals, some magazine stories, newspaper articles and reports of lectures, and scores of book reviews of philosophical works.

Books

1911 *Schopenhauer's Criticism of Kant's Theory of Experience,* New York, Longmans, Green.

1914 *Pawns of Liberty* (with Corrinne S. Tsanoff), New York, Outing (later Macmillan).

1924 *The Problem of Immortality: Studies in Personality and Value,* New York, Macmillan.

1931 *The Nature of Evil,* New York, Macmillan.
Republished selections from it:
1954 "A Gradational View of Good and Evil," in Daniel J. Bronstein & Harold M. Schulweis, eds., *Approaches to the Philosophy of Religion,* New York, Prentice-Hall, pp. 286-291.
1962 "The Nature of Evil," in Milton P. Foster, ed., *Voltaire's Candide and the Critics,* Belmont, California, Wadsworth Publ. Co., pp. 102-105.
1962 "The Nature of Evil," in George Abernethy & Thomas A. Langford, eds., *Philosophy of Religion: A Book of Readings,* New York, Macmillan, pp. 420-428.

1942 *Religious Crossroads,* New York, E. P. Dutton.

1942 *The Moral Ideals of Our Civilization,* New York, E. P. Dutton.

1947 *Ethics,* New York, Harper & Bros. (rev. ed. 1955).
Republished selections from it:
1953 "Historical Development of the Family: Social and Individual Factors," in Arthur Robert Olsen, ed., *Readings on Marriage and Social Relations,* Harrisburg, Pa., Stackpole, pp. 219-221.

1955 "La Temperance," in Armand Cuvillier, ed., *Textes Choisis des Auteurs Philosophiques,* Paris, Armand Colin, pp. 211 f.

1962 "Intellectual Freedom and Higher Education," in Wilfred S. Dowden & T. N. Marsh, eds., *The Heritage of Freedom,* New York, Harper & Bros., pp. 201-206.

1949 *The Ways of Genius,* New York, Harper & Bros.

1953 *The Great Philosophers,* New York, Harper & Bros. (second ed., New York, Harper & Row, 1964).

1962 *Worlds to Know: A Philosophy of Cosmic Perspectives,* New York, Humanities Press (English ed. entitled *Science and Human Perspectives,* London, Routledge & Kegan Paul).

Monographs

1917 "The Problem of Life in the Russian Novel," *The Rice Institute Pamphlet,* IV, No. 2, 115-272.

1922 "Aspects of Modern Pessimism," *The Rice Institute Pamphlet,* IX, No. 4, 181-295.

1928 "The Problem of Evil," *The Rice Institute Pamphlet,* XV, No. 1, 1-73.

1931 "The Beginnings of Modern Ethics," *The Rice Institute Pamphlet,* XVIII, No. 4, 200-277.

Essays In Cooperative Volumes

1917 "Freedom as an Ethical Postulate: Kant," in *Philosophical Essays in Honor of James Edwin Creighton,* New York, Macmillan, pp. 61-77.

1931 "A Gradational View of the Nature of Evil," in *Proceedings of the Seventh International Congress of Philosophy,* Oxford, Oxford University Press, pp. 393-397.

1932 "The Theory of Moral Value," in *Contemporary Idealism in America,* New York, Macmillan, pp. 217-236.

1936 "Intellectual Training and Moral Advance," in *Higher Education and Society: A Symposium,* Norman, Okla., University of Oklahoma Press, pp. 49-56.

1936 "Philosophy in Folk-Lore," in *Coyote Wisdom,* Austin, Texas Folk-Lore Society, pp. 145-154.

1939 "Folk-Lore and Tradition in a Growing Society," in *In The Shadow of History,* Austin, Texas Folk-Lore Society, pp. 1-8.

1945 "The Significance of Virtue in Moral Judgment and in Unfolding Outlook on Life," in *Essays on the Theory of Value and Valuation,* Minneapolis, Minn., Burgess, pp. 63-65.

1947 "American Life as the Testing Ground of International Coöperation," in *Conflicts of Power in Modern Culture,* New York, Harper and Bros., pp. 318-321.

1964 "The Idea of Progress in Philosophy of History," in *Memorias del XIII Congreso Internacional de Filosofia,* (Universidad Nacional Autónoma de México), VI, 457-465.

Also: "Cardinal Virtues," "Conscience," "Ethics," "Evil, Problem of," "Immortality," "Self-Realization," in *Collier's Encyclopedia,* New York, R. F. Collier and Son.

"Idealism," in *Telugu Encyclopedia,* Waltair, India.

Articles

1908 "Ivan Vazoff, Balkan Poet and Novelist," *Poet Lore,* Spring Number, 98-110.

1910 "Schopenhauer's Criticism of Kant's Theory of Ethics," *The Philosophical Review,* XIX, No. 5, 512-534.

1910 "Professor Boodin on the Nature of Truth," *The Philosophical Review,* XIX, No. 6, 632-638.

1911 "Rejoinder," *The Philosophical Review,* XX, No. 1, 63-66.

1914 "On the Psychology of Poetic Construction: An Experimental Method," *American Journal of Psychology,* XXV, 528-537.

1915 "The Relations of Philosophy and Science," *Scientific Society of San Antonio,* January, 3-12.

1915 "Bulgaria's Role in the Balkans," *The Journal of Race Development,* V, No. 3, 247-267.

1916 "Bulgaria's Part in the European War," *Current History,* V, 70-76.

1917 "The Shoulders of Atlas," (with Corrinne S. Tsanoff), *The Atlantic Monthly,* January, CXIX, No. 1, 85-92.

1918 "Bulgaria's Case," *The Journal of Race Development,* VIII, No. 3, 296-317.

1920 "The Destiny of the Self in Professor Bosanquet's Theory," *The Philosophical Review,* XXIX, No. 1, 59-79.

1920 "Immortality and Monadistic Idealism," *The Monist,* XXX, No. 2, 292-306.

1920 "Pessimism and Immortality," *The Philosophical Review,* XXIX, No. 6, 547-570.

1921 "Dante's Idea of Immortality," *The Rice Institute Pamphlet,* VIII, No. 2, 139-169.

1926 "Francis Bacon and Philosophic Thought," *The Rice Institute Pamphlet,* XIII, No. 1, 1-22.

1927 "Bulgarian Poetry as a Reflection of National Culture," *Pages from Bulgaria's Life: Year Book for 1924-1927* (The Bulgarian Student Association, New York), 1927, 76-81.

1927 "Religious Education Without Religious Bias," *Proceedings,* National Association of Principals of Schools for Girls, pp. 29-47.
1929 "Hartmann's Pessimism," *The Philosophical Review,* XXXVIII, No. 4, 350-371.
1929 "Jesus' Estimate of Man," *The Churchman,* CXL, No. 10, 10-13.
1929 "Moral Education in the Public School," *The Texas Outlook,* XIII, No. 11, 9-10, 74, 76.
1931 "How Shall a Child Find God?" *McCall's Magazine,* April, pp. 74, 77.
1932 "Goethe and Philosophy," *The Rice Institute Pamphlet,* XIX, No. 2, 61-83.
1933 "The Ethics of Spinoza," *The Rice Institute Pamphlet,* XX, No. 2, 216-237.
1940 "The Notion of Perfection," *The Philosophical Review,* XLIX, No. 1, 25-36.
1941 "Books for Children," *News Notes,* Texas Library Association, XVII, No. 3, 3-6, 9.
1942 "Conviction and Tolerance," *The Philosophical Review,* LI, No. 2, 105-123. (Republished in *Proceedings and Addresses of The American Philosophical Association,* Vol. XV.)
1942 "Literature and National Destiny in Russia," *The Rice Institute Pamphlet,* XXIX, No. 4, 336-359.
1944 "Morality in International Relations," *Rice Owl,* VII, No. 3, 5.
1944 "Blessed are Men of Right Will," *Motive,* V, No. 1, 7-8.
1948 "The Creative Arts in Texas," *Proceedings,* The Philosophical Society of Texas, XIII, 9-22.
1951 "The College Library as the Reader's Workshop," *Texas Library Journal,* XXVII, No. 1, 9-14. (Republished in part in *The Michigan Librarian,* XVII, No. 2, 14.)
1951 "Moral Principles and National Interests," *Ethics,* LXII, No. 1, 11-15.
1952 "What Should be the Relation of Morals to Law; A Round Table," *Journal of Public Law,* I, No. 2, 268-271.
1953 "Pantheism and Personal Immortality," *The Rice Institute Pamphlet,* XL, No. 1, 1-23. (Originally delivered as Foerster Lecture on Immortality at the University of California, 1951.)
1953 "Intellectual Freedom," *The Rice Thresher,* XL, No. 35, (Reprinted as a pamphlet for wide distribution and republished in a number of papers.)
1954 "Reality as Substance, Process, and Value," *The Rice Institute Pamphlet,* XLI, No. 3, 41-59.
1956 "Social Morality and the Principle of Justice," *Ethics,* LXVII, No. 1, 12-16.

1957 "The Idea of Progress," *Forum,* The University of Houston, April, pp. 25-28.

1957 "The Bulgarian Bogomiles and the Range of Their Influence," *American Bulgarian Review,* VII, No. 3, 13-15.

1958 "Ancient Classical Alternatives and Approaches to the Idea of Progress," *Greek and Byzantine Studies,* July, pp. 81-92.

1959 "Evolution, Teleology, and History," *The Rice Institute Pamphlet,* XLVI, No. 1, 32-52.

1960 "The Rice Memorial Chapel," *The Rice Institute Pamphlet,* XLVII, No. 2, 1-12.

1960 "Tragedy and Comedy: The Pendulum of Dramatic Art," *Forum,* The University of Houston, Fall and Winter, pp. 19-22.

1961 "The Meaning of Excellence," *Forum,* The University of Houston, Summer, pp. 47-50.

1962 "Enduring Values in Education," *Rice University Studies,* XLVIII, No. 2, 22-38.

1963 "Eulogy of President John F. Kennedy," *Congressional Record,* CIX, Part 19, 25043-25044. (Originally delivered at Memorial Service in the Rice University Memorial Chapel.)

1964 "Literary Art and Moral Values," *Rice University Studies,* L, No. 1, 91-103.

1965 "Intellectual Potential in Texas: Resources and Challenges," *Proceedings,* The Philosophical Society of Texas, XXVIII (1964), 5-12.